WRITING THE HARD STUFF

WRITING THE HARD STUFF

Turning Difficult Subjects into Meaningful Prose

Nicole Walker

BLOOMSBURY ACADEMIC
LONDON • NEW YORK • OXFORD • NEW DELHI • SYDNEY

BLOOMSBURY ACADEMIC
Bloomsbury Publishing Plc, 50 Bedford Square, London, WC1B 3DP, UK
Bloomsbury Publishing Inc, 1359 Broadway, New York, NY 10018, USA
Bloomsbury Publishing Ireland, 29 Earlsfort Terrace, Dublin 2, D02 AY28, Ireland

BLOOMSBURY, BLOOMSBURY ACADEMIC and the Diana logo are trademarks of Bloomsbury Publishing Plc

First published in Great Britain 2026

Copyright © Nicole Walker, 2026

Nicole Walker has asserted her right under the Copyright, Designs and Patents Act, 1988, to be identified as Author of this work.

For legal purposes, the Acknowledgments on p. viii constitute an extension of this copyright page.

Cover design by Matt Thame
Cover image © SurfsUp / Shutterstock

All rights reserved. No part of this publication may be: i) reproduced or transmitted in any form, electronic or mechanical, including photocopying, recording or by means of any information storage or retrieval system without prior permission in writing from the publishers; or ii) used or reproduced in any way for the training, development or operation of artificial intelligence (AI) technologies, including generative AI technologies. The rights holders expressly reserve this publication from the text and data mining exception as per Article 4(3) of the Digital Single Market Directive (EU) 2019/790.

Bloomsbury Publishing Plc does not have any control over, or responsibility for, any third-party websites referred to or in this book. All internet addresses given in this book were correct at the time of going to press. The author and publisher regret any inconvenience caused if addresses have changed or sites have ceased to exist, but can accept no responsibility for any such changes.

A catalogue record for this book is available from the British Library.

ISBN: HB: 978-1-3505-1866-7
PB: 978-1-3505-1865-0
ePDF: 978-1-3505-1867-4
eBook: 978-1-3505-1868-1

Typeset by RefineCatch Ltd, Bungay, Suffolk
Printed and bound in Great Britain

For product-safety-related questions, contact productsafety@bloomsbury.com.

To find out more about our authors and books, visit www.bloomsbury.com and sign up for our newsletters.

For my mom, who gets me through the hard stuff.

CONTENTS

Acknowledgments   viii

1   DIGGING INTO THE HARD STUFF   1

2   WHY HARD STUFF?   11

3   WHY RESEARCH?   27

4   WHAT HARD STUFF?   45

5   THE BRAIDED ESSAY   57

6   THE INCLUSIVENESS OF METAPHOR   75

7   OBJECT LESSONS   97

8   DISSOCIATION VERSUS DISTANCE   113

9   FINDING THE MUSIC   127

Bibliography   155
Index   159

ACKNOWLEDGMENTS

It might be easiest to just thank everyone I've ever met—not only for fear of forgetting to appreciate someone, but because writing is such a collaborative process. I want to thank every teacher I've had, every story, poem, or essay I've read, everyone who met me for wine or dinner. Writers are great sponges and this book is an attempt to show the pores of the sponge—where my thinking about how writing works and how we work through the hard things, be they personal trauma, political concern, or complicated theory, and share them as stories.

This book is an amalgam of so many people's stories and work that the index should serve as another page of gratitude. But in particular, I want to thank my writing friends, many of whom I met in graduate school and who have continued to grow and share our work together. Margot Singer, who edited two editions of *Bending Genre,* makes sure I keep one foot on the ground as I threaten to spiral off into syntactical outer space. Lynn Kilpatrick, who keeps me on an even keel, hiking and talking with me about books, breathlessly (on my part). Matthew Batt who has been writing nonfiction with me from the beginning and David McGlynn who helped me make essays into whole books. Steve Fellner, who expects me to keep refining the question "what is an essay?" Eric Burger who taught me the difference between fewer and less and yet showed me ways to write more and more. Mary Anne Mohanraj who thinks we can do anything and everything. Jeff Chapman, who hovers on my editorial shoulder, suggesting that I could be just a little bit funnier. Heidi Czerwiec who keeps the song in the story. Peter Covino who reminds me to celebrate every win.

And then there are the friends who I met after grad school who keep expanding my understanding about what writing can be. Ander Monson, who ensures I push the boundaries of nonfiction. Lawrence Lenhart, who makes sure I can perform the work as well as write it. David Carlin, whose humor and elegant writing inspires me. Ann Cummins, who taught me how to combine teaching and writing—the results of which I hope you can see here. Karen Renner, who will talk about writing with me any day, any time. David Shields, who questions everything, and Robin Hemley, who taught me about the difference between thinking you know something and knowing you know something. Katharine Coles, who brought science and literature together in lightning bolt kinds of ways. Thanks to Andrea Askowitz, Allison Langer, Jane Marks, Jane Armstrong, who helped me see the bigger context of my small story, and Megan Quinn, who helped me bridge writing and science writing—another kind of hard I tackled here. And, I deeply appreciate my students, especially those in my Fall 2024 English 379, Intermediate Creative Nonfiction Writing, who gave me feedback on an early version of the manuscript and made it stronger with their thoughtfulness, generosity, and brilliance.

I cannot thank enough the people who support the writing by giving me time and encouragement and patience as I struggle to get it right: Angie Hansen, the best chair and friend anyone could have. Bruce Hungate, Director of the Center for Ecosystem Science and Society, who gave me the space to conceive of and write this book. My incredible editors at Bloomsbury, Lucy Strong, Aanchal Vij, and Lisa Carden have been so supportive through this whole process. And also thanks to Laurie Edwards for her thoughtful review and to Matt Bell for his dear friendship and absolutely kind endorsement of the book.

And thank you, my sweet family, Erik, Zoë, Max, Mom, Paige, Valerie, Steve, Ellie, Rick, Joy, Marshall, Sue, Van, Tim, Emily, Bill, Brigg, Cameron, Lily, and Blake, and dear friends, Rebecca, Todd, Misty, Megan, and Beya, who love me so unconditionally that I sometimes have the hubris to believe I might create a good book.

Parts of this book have been published in different form in *Assay, Creative Nonfiction, Essay Daily,* and *Bending Genre.*

"*Listen to me: It is not gauche to write about trauma. It is subversive.*"
—Melissa Febos

Chapter 1

DIGGING INTO THE HARD STUFF

I want to begin by saying writing will save your life. I want to, but I won't. The first reason is that I sometimes tend toward hyperbole. Saving lives sounds dramatic. It also puts a lot of pressure on the act of writing. It might be harder to write if so much is at stake. Writing does its good work usually by being fun and creating meaning. When things are going well, writing brings meaningful joy, which can contribute to a life worth saving, but the effect of writing saving your life is corollary, not causal. Writing doesn't work like therapy. Your job is to shape your story with all the writing tools available that can give you agency over the hard stuff you're writing about. These tools are not the same tools that improve mental health, although I do believe taking agency over the hard stuff is empowering. To make art is to make meaning. To write is to connect with someone—maybe just a friend, maybe a million readers, maybe just your therapist. Maybe your mom. When you work to write about the hard things—be they personally traumatic, conceptually difficult, or sticky political subjects—the work itself provides insight into those hard things, which can be life-altering, if not lifesaving. If you make it so you express your hard things in a way that matters to others, you've opened your story. You've let others in.

Your story matters. How to make it matter to everyone else? You'll need nodes. Entries. Points of connection. How are you going to invite your reader into a world that you've been living in so long? You know the shape of your brain. You know the salient details. You know the flashes of image and story. How can you convey your interiority with equal parts clarity and emotion? But to gain distance and understanding, you may need to use the tools of dissociating from your subject through language, research, an extra-terrestrial point of view. To make the emotional experience available, you'll have to get down into the dirt.

Writing the Hard Stuff provides a road map for writers who want to dig deeply into issues and experiences that require special craft techniques to make the writing experience bearable, maybe even joyful, and make that material more accessible to the reader. The "hard stuff" includes writing about traumatic events like domestic violence and sexual abuse, but it also includes political, scientific, cultural, environmental, and other thorny subjects.

I have seen ways people have worked with their hard subject through many writing strategies from metaphor to research, through the lens of a specific object to strict formal choices. This book isn't a step-by-step textbook. What I want to do is show you how digging deeply into hard experiences, hard thoughts, hard ideas may allow you to connect with readers, to connect big ideas, to connect your hard stories to the hard stories that you've read and heard. I want to ask, what is resonant to you? How can you make your hard story resonate with others?

As a touchstone for what I consider hard stuff, I refer to an essay in the *New York Times* I published in August 2022, two months after *Roe* was overturned, called "My Abortion at 11 Wasn't a Choice. It Was My Life."

On August 17, 2022, two months after the *Dobbs* decision came down from the Supreme Court, I wrote for the *New York Times*, "I predict that my 17-year-old daughter will become a doctor. When my husband told her about a neuroscientist and nutritionist he met while producing a documentary, she said, 'That sounds like the job for me.' She knows everything about the gut biome, dopamine and herniated discs. She does not look away at times when others might—like when my mother unexpectedly texted me pictures of a cyst she had removed from the back of her head, sitting bloody in a specimen cup. 'That's exactly what I would do,' my daughter said. "You have to show people."

I don't mind looking at such things, though I would like a little warning. But here, I offer no warning, except to say that in an alternate world—one without *Roe v. Wade*—the above conversation with my daughter would not have happened. In fact, my family and I would not have our lives together at all. Our loss is collective, but this story is mine. I ask you not to look away.

> In 1982, when I was 10 years old, a 14-year-old boy molested me. He was supposed to be babysitting me and my younger sisters. After the twins went to sleep, the babysitter and I sat on the couch, watching "M*A*S*H," which came on after the news. He started caressing my arm. Then my neck. Then he took off my shirt and my pants. Then his clothes. He lay on top of me and had intercourse with me. I had a vague idea of what was happening. My parents had been forthcoming about how babies were made, and during long and lazy summers in

the suburbs of Salt Lake City, I watched plenty of instructive soap operas.

I didn't really know how wrong the babysitter situation was. I was flattered by the attention, but also confused. Why me? What does this mean? Was he my boyfriend? Why did we have to keep it a secret?

He continued to molest me for more than a year. I haven't always used the word "molest"—I felt too much guilt and complicity. I am still prone to feeling both. I'm not sure if that's a product of the molestation, or if that is my personality, or if the two can even be disentangled.

When I was 11, he impregnated me. I use the active verb, with me as direct object, intentionally. To "get pregnant" suggests he threw the baseball and I, knowing it was coming, caught it. I did not mean to catch anything, nor did I know how to avoid doing so. My mom, who was already worried that something seemed wrong, figured it out. "Are you pregnant?" she asked me. I nodded yes. How did she know? I barely knew. Maybe she noticed my absent period, or maybe it was pure motherly intuition.

In 1983, abortion was legal in Utah because it was legal across the United States. I did not feel lucky to get an abortion. I felt like garbage. The babysitter did not have to go to the clinic. The babysitter was not shunned and censured by our community; most people didn't even know what he had done. Only my mom and I were subject to the shame of entering that special building for that special procedure. Although no one in the neighborhood or at school talked to me about it, I could feel the electric gossip surge around me. I eventually skipped a grade.

In many parts of the world, the US included, adult men marry children, sometimes legally and sometimes not. These girls, some of them the age that I was when I was molested, are sometimes forced to give birth. The pelvis can be too small for the fetus to pass through during birth. The fetus often dies. The girl can suffer fistula, where the pressure during labor rips a hole between the wall of the bladder or rectum and the vagina. Bodily waste then drips through the vagina instead of out its proper vents.

Some abortion rights supporters worry that devoting too much energy to the stories of young children who need abortions—abortions that are still legal in at least some US states—narrows the cause. Focusing on these exceptional cases, they fear, could shift the fight away from a more expansive battle for women's rights and the obvious truth that bodily autonomy should exist for all people.

But I am telling you all this—even though it hurts to say, even I speed over my words as I tell this story in an attempt to get past this as quick as I can— because the world changed on June 24, 2022. On that day, I understood the extent of what we were losing.

The "freedom to choose" wasn't what I experienced in 1984. My abortion wasn't a choice. It was my life. If I had been forced to give birth, I wouldn't be texting my mom from my home in a beautiful mountain town. I wouldn't teach at the nearby university. I wouldn't be working on a book about climate change and how to shatter predetermined destinies. I wouldn't be married to my husband or have my two children. My life would not have been my own. I would be a prisoner subject to a body's whims — and not *my* body's whims, but the whims of a teenage boy who, as best I can tell, experienced no consequences for inflicting what his body wanted upon my own.

On June 24, I felt the prison gates fall around me, around my daughter, around everyone with a uterus. Pregnancy and childbirth change life trajectories.

I wrote, "Now, for many more Americans, trajectories are set. Paths defined. This future is foreseeable. I ask that you look at it."

The essay found a large readership. I didn't necessarily want to tell the story. I didn't necessarily want my mom to have to answer the questions the fact-checking editors asked about whether I was eleven or twelve when it happened. I didn't necessarily want to be called brave for sharing my story. But, almost two months after the Dobbs decision which overturned the constitutional protection for pre-viability abortion confirmed in *Roe v. Wade*, I felt compelled to write it. This story was hard to write both in terms of the trauma and the politics that surrounded it. I was afraid I would become a target for anti-choice believers. I felt exposed about my personal story and afraid the politics I presented would bring public ridicule.

But that didn't happen. By talking about how my daughter wanted to be a neuroscientist, how my mom had recently had a cyst from her scalp removed, and by admitting it was hard to write about this even forty years later, I used several of the strategies I offer that I will discuss more fully in later chapters. The context I provided about my daughter, the weird detail I included about my mom's cyst, the immediacy of the emotion I admitted to were, in retrospect, craft tools that gave me emotional distance from the events and provided enough specific details to allow readers to enter the story.

I was worried that when the piece came out, people would be sending me death threats or burning my house down. But instead, people reached out to me. They thanked me. The connections I made transformed my relationship to what had happened to me. It felt like that in an instant, all the shame I'd felt for having been sullied, duped, and ostracized disappeared. The word "abortion" didn't signal spoilage or damage or scum, but became a word like "healthcare" and "medicine." Because I could shape my story on my own terms, whatever detritus that had attached to me from the molestation or the abortion fell away. It was my story to tell—and telling it to a million readers was the most empowering moment of my life.

Shortly after the essay came out in the *New York Times*, I was invited to give a workshop on writing about abortion during a week of reproductive rights activism and mobilization. In that workshop, hosted by the Flagstaff Abortion Alliance and other local rights groups, I met with that group of ten on a Sunday morning in a cinder block building. One woman told us we were the first people she had ever told, other than medical staff, that she'd had an abortion. Another woman told us about her pre-*Roe* abortion in 1969. I told them that the workshop was about writing the hard things—be it complicated personal stories or difficult, potentially divisive social issues. Abortion is a difficult subject matter not only on a personal level but a social one. It is drenched in politics and suffused in partisan argument. But it's also hard to write about head-on. On the one hand, it's just like writing about a cyst or a broken arm, which might make for a boring story. Millions of people have had abortions. What makes yours unique? How do you convey how difficult it might have been to go against your culture, religion, or family? What does it mean to lose the right to body autonomy? How does that hit you in the physical gut? How does your loss of rights resonate with others?

To access their unique stories, I had each of these workshop participants write a paragraph about something they'd been obsessed with this summer, adding as many sensory details as possible. They could write about any topic of which they had some knowledge and had been on their mind: aspen trees, pasta, volcanoes, chickens, eggs, or trying to grow tomatoes in Flagstaff's uncooperative climate. I then asked them to time-write their own, harder stories, which could be their personal experience or their insight into the political moment. For two minutes, they wrote about their troubled or troubling stories, their abortion or their feelings about *Roe* being overturned, then they switched to their obsession for three minutes. Then, after three minutes, they went back to their personal story. The effect of this "toggling" serves several purposes—it gives the writing tension. It gives the author sensory material to dip into. And it gives the author a chance to escape the hard story for a couple of minutes. It allows for perspective, distance, and authority because one is rooting one's opinion and personal experience in shared, objective facts. It also allows for images, sounds, details to emerge that resonate across both stories.

The tools I suggest for writing about emotionally and topically difficult subjects work well for subjects that are politically difficult. The *New York Times* piece was personal *and* political. As you'll have seen, I pleaded to the readers that although my story was hard to hear, to please not look away. I was surprised by the lines I wrote about closing my laptop as my husband walked by. How strange to be able to write to a million readers and still feel shame at the thought of my husband seeing the words on the cold, hard screen. To write across ideas stretches the choices beyond right or left, one or the other, and instead to see the elasticity of thought. "Resistance" is important to the idea because it describes the way metaphor helps challenge the stultified pathways of our neural networks. Two ideas. One time. It's important because the brain resists new ways of thinking. It's important because resistance is an effective political tool.

This book offers craft techniques and examples for writers to use as they move more deeply into difficult topics. I don't believe trauma, pain, or political opinions are necessary for good writing, but I do believe texture and depth are. We all have stories that are hard to share— it is due to that difficulty that the stories we write find resonant moments in the struggle between these interior narratives and external ones.

As Adrienne Rich wrote, "the personal is political." That doesn't mean that every personal story has a one-to-one relationship to the political. Although the short essay I wrote about my abortion was directly in response to the Supreme Court overturning *Roe*, the book I've written, *How to Plant a Billion Trees*, tackles not only the politics of reproductive freedom, but also the politics of environmental stewardship. Forests serve as a model of how shared resources create a stable environment. I pair my story of a potentially 'ruined' child who became reintegrated into a system of family, friends, and community. As I investigated my affinity for forests while trying to understand how I ended up at least 50 percent mentally stable, I found parity between how forests support each other with the help of mycorrhizal fungi, these vast, underground system of tiny threads called hyphae that transfer nutrients from healthy trees to disadvantaged ones.

1. Digging into the Hard Stuff

It might have been simpler to just tell my story: a young girl growing up in a dominantly Mormon community was molested by her babysitter who impregnated her. After undergoing an abortion, she feels cut off from her family. The babysitter's sister was one of the few friends she had. She dove into Salt Lake City's punk subculture, where she found refuge with other marginalized kids. But, over time, she began to reconnect with her family and to build a community that doesn't see her as ruined.

But that story doesn't examine the nuances of how that reintegration happened or why it mattered. The straightforward story belies not only emotion but meaning. How can I convey the trouble to my reader? How can I explain why I return to this subject in so much of my writing? How can I tie this story to the larger narratives of sex abuse, abortion rights, and cultural disaffection? To develop as many connection points as possible to explain the nuances, I needed to use formal devices. I might even call them constraints. To make the story bigger, I needed some boundaries.

The braided essay requires a writer to toggle back and forth between two or more subjects. One paragraph describes, say, a personal experience and the next paragraph describes the intelligence of squid. By researching squid, I'm creating a framework for my personal story. Other constraints might include something as binding as a sonnet, with its fourteen lines of iambic pentameter and strict rhyme or a pantoum with its second and fourth lines of each stanza repeating as the first and third lines of the next stanza, and the first line of the poem is the last line of the final stanza, and the third line of the first stanza is the second of the final. These restraints can catalyze creativity. As chef Savannah Miller says before the season 21 finale of *Top Chef*, "The way my brain works, if I have too many choices, I have issues." Or, as the punk band Nomeansno sang, "Tie up my hands with your chains/they are bound to set me free." Or, as St. Augustine wrote in *City of God*, Book 19, Chapter 17: "If, therefore, we are bound to God, then we are bound to the highest good, and thus, this bondage is indeed the truest freedom." While I don't subscribe to a particular religion, I do think there is something freeing in binding yourself to your art, to the material of the world, to some self-imposed rules that let your story emerge. By pairing my story with the story of the forest, I have not only metaphors available to dip into, but bounds around my own story that, I hope, keep me from melodrama, invigorate my word choice and syntax, and provide multiple entrees into the narrative.

I will show you how I have used, and how other authors have used, formal strategies to provide distance, context, and multiple entry points for writer to shape difficult content, making it more accessible to the reader. Although I draw on my own work because it is the work most available to me, I highlight the work of many other authors, mostly nonfiction writers as well as a few fiction writers and poets, who look toward formal strategies to express the full significance of their stories. I take the word "express" literally. As one places narrative next to narrative, new meaning emerges, like pressing oil from olives.

I am one of those writers who loves not only *having* written, but the act of writing. I love to make wild metaphors, to envision scenes, to remember details from when I was three or four like the plastic yellow horse with a blue mane that I rode around and around my grandma's neighborhood sidewalk until I hit an uneven square and bounced off my horse and onto the concrete where I busted open my lip. Later, my grandmother fed me slices of apples with salt on them. The whole scene in my memory blasts forward in full color—yellow, blue, blood red, apple red. I can see the salt dissolving tiny craters into white flesh. I can taste the sweet and salty liquid. I cannot help to make a metaphor between blood and salty apple flesh. I will use those sensory images to try to plumb deeper into the story. Where were my parents? Were they angry when they came to pick me up that my grandma had allowed me to fall? Did they suspect she'd been drinking? Later, on a different visit, one where I was to spend the night, my grandma, who drank bourbon and coffee most of the day and into the night, fell down the stairs at her house on Melbourne Street. Who called the ambulance? Where were my parents? Were they angry when they came to pick me up that my grandma had fallen down the stairs? She could have died. And then who would have taken care of me?

This is a hard story for me to write because I want to protect my grandmother, whom I loved. I also want to protect my mom, who might not want to remember the story—perhaps she feels like she never should have left me with my dad's mom. It's hard because alcoholism runs in my family. As someone who still drinks wine, writing about alcohol is tricky. When does regular drinking become abuse? Perhaps I'm protecting the booze!

Since I am reluctant to name or limit what might be difficult for you to write, I share my story as an example. I also want to share the ways I protected myself from reliving the hard stuff as I wrote it. And, finally, I want to show how pairing that personal hard with another narrative— be it scientific research, another person's story, or a metaphor—offers multiple access points for readers. Maybe a reader hasn't experienced the same difficult experiences as I have, but maybe, if I were to expand the grandmother-falling story, the reader may find their way into my story with their interest in the science of salt's corrosive abilities, an appley/Fall allusion to Adam and Eve's story, or to my mom's version of how they picked me up as the EMTs rolled my grandmother into the ambulance. The story, written closely, provides the details. The details provide the access.

As a teacher of nonfiction writing, I have had the privilege to work with students from many backgrounds who often have difficult stories to tell. I am not alone in hewing to formal strategies. It is a well-known writing adage to say that one needs distance from one's material to write it well. Usually, by distance, we mean time. I agree that distance is required to shape the hard stuff successfully, but time isn't the only distancing tool available. Each chapter will provide a strategy to attain a kind of distance so the writer can tell their story and can connect to the larger issues attendant to that hard stuff.

You will find ways to write that help unearth stories that may be difficult to tell and to tell them without asking the writer suffering anew by offering writers strategies of how to build moments within the text where they may rest, detach, detour, distract, change points of view, or duck into entirely different content.

In nonfiction courses, I work with students to hone their prose, clarify semantics, rethink syntax, sketch fully-fledged scenes, refine dialogue, and add detail. But the harder work lies is helping writers to find ways for their individual stories to connect with readers. Many of my graduate, undergraduate, and community-based workshop students write about hard, often terrible, things like molestation, the death of loved ones, suicide, and domestic abuse. Sometimes, they write so quickly over their trauma that the reader barely understands what happened in the narrative. How can I ask these writers to stay with their hard story and add detail and dialogue to something that is already so upsetting? Instead of asking them to necessarily stay in that hard place, I suggest ways students might complement the hard things by adding detailed information, research, change of perspective, and metaphor to their essays. As the student works back and forth between the interior hard stuff and these exterior topics, not only are they able to gain some distance from that difficult material, but they also find parallel stories in the external world. The effects are that the writer gains perspective on their personal story and the reader gains access to the story through multiple entry points—through interior or exterior doors, to add a metaphor.

Writing the Hard Stuff is organized into chapters that show how certain strategies work in my and other author's writing. Readers of this book may use it to experiment with each strategy, pairing different hard-to-tackle stories with different techniques. Or, the users of this book might use each of the strategies to write about the one hard thing they've struggled to write about. I see this text as a challenge to write the hard stuff, as a guide for how the writer might do it, and to serve a sympathetic bouncing board, as its author has struggled through how to write this hard stuff too.

The strategies include chapters on how to write braided essays, view a subject through various lenses, experiment with spatial and temporal distance, free-associate, invoke metaphors, and to provide formal structures upon which writers can scaffold hard stories, troubling experiences, as well as complicated theories and politics. Each of these chapters—writing through metaphor, objects, and associations—constitutes a kind of a braid, which is I begin with a general version for the braided essay and then follow that chapter with different approaches that build on the form of the braided essay.

I hope these strategies help you garner whatever distance necessary for you to see your story both as important and to shape that story into something that readers can access from many vantage points. Some of them may serve to protect your mental and emotional well-being, but each promise to broaden the reach of these personal stories by connecting the interiority of the personal story with the exterior world.

Chapter 2

WHY HARD STUFF?

Things that make me feel ashamed or gross, confused or incompetent, are hard for me to write about. This includes abortion and molestation as well as habitat loss, species extinction, my cat Zane who is lost and probably not coming back, tooth pain, my husband, the apple cider industry, eggs, school vouchers, the impact of lying, the bend of a river, and how all water is actually dinosaur pee. I want to say, well, those things are everything, but that's not quite true. I love to write about garbage, brine shrimp, my kids, mycorrhizal fungi. I love it, but it's still hard.

I find it easy to write about only one thing: my kids. And that probably shouldn't be easy. But I spent a lot of my life trying to get to see the world from their points of view. I wanted to be the kind of mother who asked, what do you think? I think kids know a lot—maybe even more than adults. And yet, they also drive me crazy with their stubborn ways. In between this deep admiration and frustration, I like to work out my love for them on the page—which they generously have let me do. It's important to know when my story stops and theirs begins. I want to honor their privacy, but I also want to write about the stories we share so we have them forever. Also, my children make me laugh and maybe, if I write their stories well, others will laugh with us. For example, when my son Max, at thirteen, had a basketball game at his middle school. He left his backpack in the lobby because, I think, he believed that because it was *his* school, his stuff was safe wherever he put it. Dear reader, it was not safe. I could tell when we left the gym for the lobby that something was wrong. His face fell. He looked around nervously. Because I am the finder in my household, I know the look. Something is missing. But this was a big thing. His iPhone was in that backpack. Max didn't want to ask for help out loud. Finally, he confesses that he can't find his backpack. We look everywhere. Under the bleachers. In the bathrooms. In the other gym. We cannot find it anywhere. We give up. I'm yelling the whole time about how Max needs to get it together. Max ignores my complaining. He's hatching a plan. This is an excerpt from a longer piece about the lost iPhone of 2022.

"I have an idea. Let me have your phone." He takes my phone from me, which doubles as my wallet, which is why my son and daughter call me "Boomer" and laugh their Gen Z heads off. I am Gen X, I shout to them, but, like the rest of the world, they don't believe Gen X exists.

"What if we try this?" He pushes Find My Phone on my cell. A ping. A pulse. A light of hope and we are off to the races, driving 90 miles per hour on Highway 89 while Max yells, "They've stopped at a light." Or "They're right by Chipotle."

"Max. Max," I panic. "What if they're going all the way to Utah? How could you leave your phone in your backpack? How could you leave your backpack in the hallway? I know you think Flagstaff is 100% safe but it's just not."

We keep up the chase. Max says, "They turned left." It's Campbell Road. I've been down this road before.

I take a left, going 50 down a dirt road. We pass my former student, Dennis's, house. I wave to the chickens I met when he had me over for dinner.

Max yells, "They took a right." I speed up. "Here?"

"No, next one. Oh. God. They've stopped."

"Oh good, we'll be able to block them in," I saw more breezily than I feel.

What I've pictured happening is some lanky, early mustachioed ninth-graders watching Max as he tucked his phone into his backpack and then placed the backpack by the front door. Teenagers, smelling weakness and lithium, possessing the skills necessary to hack behind passcode, firewall, locked phone, sauntered up to the backpack as one of them slung it on his back like it was his own. Am I brave enough to tangle with surly ninth-graders? I may be older, but I will be forever shorter than that age group.

A black Suburban passes us going the other way. "Mom! They're driving away!" How could they drive away? How could they have stopped and got started again? We haven't even seen their faces yet! There's a stop sign but I only slow to look both ways. Why are they driving so fast? Probably because they think we're onto them. They're going to drive us until we run out of gas. They have a Suburban with a 40-gallon tank or something. My hybrid Rav-4 can go pretty far on a tank of gas, but not 40 gallons' worth.

The Suburban is ahead of us at the stop sign. I'm sure we will be able to catch up since it's hard to take a left on Highway 89. I assume they're heading north to the vast, open spaces of the Navajo Nation. Perhaps they don't have a full tank. Perhaps they'll have to stop in Cameron for gas and there, with many witnesses about, I can confront them.

But they don't turn left. They turn right, back toward town. I turn and follow. I'm right behind them now, honking my horn and flashing my lights. Everyone is looking at me, but I don't care. Finally, we hit the light on Saddle Springs. There is room for me to pull up next to them. I turn to look. In the driver's seat sits a Diné woman, my age, looking afraid and confused at why this white woman is yelling at her. A boy, younger than Max, sits in the backseat, looking a little afraid.

I motion for her to roll down her window.
"You have my son's phone! It's in his backpack." The light changes and she pulls away, possibly with the intention of fleeing from this yelling lady. But she does not floor it. She gently pulls to the shoulder.
"Max. Get out. Go get your phone." I'm afraid I will look crazy if I go talk to her, which might make her more nervous and drive off. Max comes back to the car with his backpack.
"He just took it by mistake. His backpack is black too."
Now, I worry about who took this other kid's black backpack.
"You got your phone?" I ask.
He takes it from a pocket. "Yeah." He pulls up TikTok.
I say, "That was nuts."
How can I be mad at a kid who was born in Flagstaff and thinks the world is pretty safe, and, at least in this case, it is.

I had a lot of fun writing this, but it is not a big story. It's a semi-entertaining anecdote where the work required was one of pacing, intentional inclusion of detail: The color of the backpacks, the ubiquity of Chipotle, my former student's chickens. And, there is intentional exclusion of detail. I said a hundred times to Max in real life, "Max. You can't keep losing stuff!" In my rendition, I do not include every single time I swore at the other cars standing between us and this tiny, expensive phone.

This is an unserious short essay, the kind of which I have to write sometimes. Not everything I write must blow someone's mind or be seen as great art or uncover the depth and breadth of the human condition. But this story is a one-off. It's true and maybe, at moments, funny but it's not part of a bigger project. When I take on bigger projects, I know I'll need to confront some hard personal history, world history, science, emotion, and cultural observations. I could avoid all that difficulty and write short essays about my kids for the rest of my life. I find my children endlessly charming, if hellbent on losing their own heads if they weren't attached. But something makes me want to plumb further depths. I believe that something is curiosity.

Although while writing the longer version of this, I learned a little about Flagstaff's building codes and how to spell Townsend Road, I didn't learn much about myself, whether it is a kind of OCD to need to find whatever is lost, or my freestyle parenting. If I wanted to take this story to another level, I could put pressure on any of those ideas. I could use the idea of speed limits as a metaphor for how I am hardwired to be the soft mother who doesn't get too mad when her kid loses a $1,000 minicomputer. I could delve into the fact that Flagstaff is seen by many Diné as a border town—the city being not particularly hospitable to people from the Navajo Nation.

Writing the hard stuff requires a kind of curiosity that is uncomfortable. There are a lot of things I don't want to know about myself. Is it racist to note that the driver of the Suburban was Diné? Did calling a kid mustachioed call negative attention to a boy's early puberty? How much hubris did it take for me to drive 90 mph on a 55-mph road? Perhaps it's not only curiosity but also a stubborn insistence that my perspective is only one one-millionth of ways the story might have played out.

When I write personal essays, I want to take that very narrow perspective and try to multiply it. How did I become who I am? How did any of us find a perspective to cling to? If I look at the situation from many points of view, might I be able to answer, at least temporarily, the big question essays often ask: How do we know the things we think we know? My attempt in writing the hard stuff is that, as with tectonic plates, with enough pressure, something meaningful may be extruded. It might even blow up, like a volcano or a geyser. Perhaps, I will see how the larger system that made Max, made me, made the kid grab the wrong backpack, made Flagstaff a border town, made a place that seemed safe in its provinciality, be seen for what it is: a burgeoning mountain town that keeps more people out, because of income-inequality, classism, racism, waterism (we're running out of water in the southwest) than it lets in.

There are good reasons to write the hard stuff:

2. Why Hard Stuff?

My first reason is that the hard stuff niggles at me. Since I was molested, I feel like there's another nervous system ghost-running alongside my original nervous system. If triggered, that ghost system kicks into action, pulsing poison. This poison manifests in a panic attack or seething at my husband for acting like the police when he interrupts me when I'm working on my book to ask who our insurance company is, or raging at drivers who refuse to justly merge or becoming uncontrollably sad when a man carries a fawn he hit with his car by her tiny legs, entrails dripping. If I pay attention to what is niggling at me with my regular nervous system by noting the triggers on paper, I can see them in perspective, recognizing that my husband isn't suggesting that I'm his secretary, that other cars are allowed on the highway, and that the driver didn't mean to hit the fawn. Writing the hard stuff forces you to slow down. Slowing down helps you connect the nodes between ghost systems and nervous systems, letting you see them in specific relief, allowing you to touch them, massage them, and sing to them.

Knowing oneself is necessary to know the world. Figuring out what we know is one reason we write. By writing our stories, we get to shape them. And, we don't have to keep them buried anymore. A common response to hard experiences is to avoid them—to stow them in a part of your brain that you don't plan to visit. I've tamped down some traumatic events, embarrassments, or confusing ideas so deep, I barely know they're there. It's fine to leave things buried but, perhaps, somewhere in your mind or heart, you know you'd do better by yourself to air these events. In pulling up some of that detritus and shaping it, not necessarily because it's healing, although it may be, your own weird/bad/complicated/untenable experiences may themselves serve as a lens through which you might view this weird/bad/complicated/untenable world. Maybe using that helps you see not only the way your brain works but the way the world works too.

Another reason to write the hard stuff is that by doing so, you can connect this wonky nervous system to the big mycorrhizal network of humanity. Community is a web of individual nodes conferring with each other. I want my hard story to meet *your* hard story. I want us to share in the tragedy and the honesty of our experience. Stories feel like the little hyphae that reach out from spore to spore. We tell our stories. We grow our network. We contribute to the health of the forest floor.

If the ghost nervous system sounds too eerie and metaphorical, imagine the way resistance to authoritarian forces worked. During the Nazi occupation of Poland, Jewish resistance forces used connected tunnels through which they shared information. Between April and

May 1943, from the tiny 1.3 square miles of land allotted to the Warsaw ghetto, Jewish insurgents operating from underground networks of bunkers and tunnels, fought the first major urban rebellion of the war.[1] In another example of networks, connections, and webs, Colson Whitehead manifested a literal underground railroad in his eponymous novel. The work of shepherding enslaved people to freedom worked by secreting letters to those trying to escape, making a figurative, not a literal underground railroad—boxcar connections by word, not steel. And, as we remember from the symbolic connections traced in *A Tale of Two Cities*, Madame Defarge knit her resistance into a blanket of revolution. Writing is connecting, and sometimes those connections lead to palpable change.

I don't mean to hyperbolize here. The personal story is not tantamount to Jewish Resistance to the Holocaust, the subversive and successful work of freeing enslaved people, or staging a revolution. But each hard story does amount to a person's story of experience and, as we write these stories, they compound that resonance. This cumulative effect is one reason I don't try to list in this book all the possible traumas and destructed lives that any of us may have encountered because first, I could not possibly list them all, second, my troubles are my stories and your troubles are your stories—I don't want to impede or determine what is hard for you—and third, if many of our stories are the result of systematic oppression, repression, explicit or implicit, every story makes a dent in that regime's armor.

When I was writing *How to Plant a Billion Trees*, a book based on the *New York Times* essay, I thought the subject of sexual abuse and abortion was too big to handle. I had been writing about forests and mycorrhizal fungi, braiding those essays with stories about how, growing up in Salt Lake City, Utah where, as a non-Mormon, I felt outcast. As word of my abortion and molestation spread, I became further outcast in Utah. Wounds began to fester. But in a forest, there is no such thing as festering. As trees and plants fall down and decay, mycorrhizal fungi feed on that decay and transform it back into nutrients for the trees. As I wrote about both subjects separately, I began to thread connections between how forests reclaim and heal themselves, but I hadn't made the connection between forest health and trauma recovery. Each thread flopped lazily because neither had any formal scaffolding—the two stories hadn't been set against each other.

Seeking editorial assistance, I sent the manuscript to my friend Jane Armstrong who lives in Normandy. She read it the same month as the United States Supreme Court overturned *Roe v. Wade*. She and I met over Zoom to discuss her thoughts about the book. The first thing she said when she came online was, "You must take this story and write an Op-Ed. Preferably for the *Times*." I had some previous success publishing with the *New York Times* for the Climate Section and for Modern Love. It was worth a shot. I wrote a draft, whose beginning buried the lede. I focused on the jpeg my mom had texted me that very morning of the back of her head where she'd had a large cyst removed. I was trying to make a metaphor about cysts and the removal of cells, but comparing an embryo to a cyst was an example of me avoiding the hard stuff by making light of it. For the *NYT*, you must arrive at the real subject quickly. I had 1,500 words to tell this hard story and to tell it well enough to feel like I had made a tiny scratch in the 150,000-pound boulder of a Supreme Court ruling that steamrolled people with uteruses. I was nervous to write about abortion for a large audience. Sometimes, I joke to my students that it's always safe to write about your family in lyric essays—we publish them in such small venues that it's unlikely our parents will read them. Not so the *New York Times*. In the article itself, I talk about the hard work of writing about it.

The hardest part of writing the essay was the moment that my husband saw me write it. His presence made the potential publicity real. I worried about the backlash he or my kids might receive. And, I hated reminding him that this had happened to me. It's one thing for me to bear the burden of feeling ruined, but I didn't want to remind him that I had been ruined, even if it was a very long time ago and true only in my head. But he's never been anything but supportive. He has never once brought up in a fight the words, "You're so fucked up because of what happened to you." Other boyfriends in the past had said such things. Erik never even intimated it. But it's not easy for him to hear about. I wanted to protect him from all the knowing that was about to happen. But whenever I ask him if I should do any of this work to stand up for bodily autonomy, from writing an essay, a whole book, or a craft book about it, or being interviewed and filmed for advertisement campaigns to protect reproductive rights, he says, "I 100 percent have your back." Being married to such a supportive partner shouldn't feel like a surprise, but it is. And it's a gift.

The fact that the ruling of the Supreme Court forced me to write this at all felt like another heavy burden. But I did indeed have to do it for political and personal reasons—which is why I write most of the time—although this piece would be published in one of the most read newspapers in the world. Publishing this piece was unlike anything I'd ever done. Sometimes, when I write about a hard subject, I write it quickly and then send it out for publication as if the essay were a hot potato and I'm handing it off to a reader who hands it off to another reader, then an editor, and then, if I'm lucky, onto readers, who can hold the potato because it has finally cooled. When I write so quickly, I barely digest my own words. But this experience required fact-checking. This required that I reread the words. It required several phone calls and questions, like: did the babysitter's parents know? And for how many years did the molestation continue? And, what did the doctors at the abortion clinic say to you? Then, the editors wanted to fact-check the essay with my mother. The hardest thing, harder than anything I'd written, was asking my mother if the editors could interview her. I called. "Mom, are you up for doing this?" To which she said, "Sure." Which was hard to read. I knew she would be nervous. I knew it would bring some trauma up for her. But, I took the "sure" as a yes because my mom believes in the idea that your rights extend to the very surface of your skin. No one has a right to dictate what happens to that skin or anything that happens behind it, she had always told me.

It's one thing to put your story out into the world. It's another to ask your mother to help you do it. Especially if some of the pushback may be directed at her. I desperately wanted to be in on the call with the editors, but that might have tainted how she answered, so I waited until she called me to tell me how it went. I asked her how she felt. She told me, "They were very nice. I said that you were eleven, not twelve. I remember because that was the year of the floods." That year, Salt Lake City's mountains had been pounded with snow. The spring melt came fast and hard, turning State Street into a river. Strangely, I have written several essays about the flood but had never written one weaving together the story of the river with the story of the abortion. Talk about hiding from our own stories.

I had such a strong feeling of wanting to protect my mother. To run away from this *NYT* business and just go back to thinking I had been twelve and hoping my mother never thought about the abortion. Instead, on the call with me, she continued, "I'm still mad they wouldn't let me go into the procedure room with you." I didn't say, that would have been so awkward, mom. I joked instead, "With Dobbs, no one gets to go into the procedure room at all now." Utah, where my mom still lives, had a trigger ban in effect the moment *Roe* was overturned to ban abortion completely. The Supreme Court has stayed that ban, allowing abortions up to eighteen weeks, but the legislature is working hard to prohibit abortion entirely. I imagined myself at age eleven, being forced to give birth to a baby. I have a hard time looking at eleven-year-olds that way but when I do, I feel nauseated. Eleven-year-old bodies, even ones that have begun to hit puberty, are still so very small. I thought of my mom having to be in the delivery room with me, at age eleven. I thought of my mom signing papers to give the baby up for adoption, because I would have been too young to sign them myself.

I cannot stay with these emotions very long, but it's important that I at least stop by and check in once in a while. This story matters not because it's unique, but because it's one of many. It matters because stories like this were kept quiet. The idea of being pro-abortion sounded worse than callous, it sounded cruel. Now that I've become deeply involved into the reproductive rights movements, I am happy to be around people who say "abortion" as loud and proud as they can.

My mom has always been an advocate for reproductive freedom. She volunteered for the League of Women Voters through most of my childhood. She signed up with the nonprofit Zero Population Growth to send money and to volunteer. Once, when I was about eight, as she was taking me and my sisters to the pediatrician, we entered an elevator with a woman and a baby. She glared so hard at the woman, I thought the woman would turn to stone. But she got off the elevator, unstony, even if she'd registered my mom's extra judgmental look.

"Why do you hate her, mom?"

"That woman is like sixteen. With a baby."

I understood something fundamental. That I was not to have a baby before I graduated from college at least. Unfortunately, I've inherited a similar judgmental scowl. I usually reserve it for people with four to ten children. I've read Zero Population Growth's mission is short-sighted, racist, and not necessary because the population should plateau on its own at 9 billion humans, and yet, it's bred in my bones that the world cannot handle four, five, six resource-sucking American children per family. My mom couldn't believe it when she had twins. "I always believed two children to replace the parents and that was enough. I didn't mean to have three." It's truly not her fault that the zygote divided in half. She made up for it by becoming the first person in our neighborhood to separate her trash and take it to the recycling center.

It's unsurprising that she felt the world overcrowded from the get-go. She was raised in a house with thirteen people: her grandma's eight children, my grandma's three daughters, and my great-grandparents. In the house my mom's grandparents on her dad's side procured for her and her sisters, after the whole family moved in, the one bathroom, on the second floor, held a clawfoot tub. The bathing policy was that the eldest, my great-grandpa, took the first bath in clean water. The water, expensive and scarce, wasn't changed. The next grown-ups, then my mom's uncles and aunts, took baths in that same water. My mom and my aunts then slid into that greasy, gritty water. They probably entered the bath cleaner than when they exited. So, I don't begrudge my mom's resistance to an overabundance of humans.

But as much of an advocate for abortion as she was, we didn't talk about it often. The most she ever said was, "I wish they'd let me in the procedure room," time and again. From the *New York Times* fact-checker, I also discovered that although the parents of the fifteen-year-old denied he molested me, they did pay for half of the abortion. $300 from his family. $300 from mine.

Because there is so much shame attached to abortion, I felt gross, sullied, unfit for company. Not only an outcast, but a social leper, a ruined human. I felt so bad for my dad and mom, and for my sisters. I felt like they shouldn't have to live with such a pariah—that my outcast state was contagious. I wanted to protect them. If I wanted to go into some deep psychology, maybe I displaced the care I would have had to take for a child onto the care I took for my family. Unfortunately, my caretaking involved removing myself from the family. I found boyfriends who knew my story, and both took advantage of my already-ruined status and my need to hide away from my shame.

The day the essay was published, the comments opened with a flood. One woman found my NAU email and offered to provide protection for me in case I was threatened. That made me nervous that things could get bad, but there were no threats. Mainly, people thanked me for sharing my story and were sorry for what had happened to me at such a young age—so many embracing words. But there were negative comments about my parents asserting that my mom and dad should have pressed changes. That had really never occurred to me. I spent many years calling what happened "sexual interference," not molestation. Not rape. I imagine my parents would have thought a court trial would make the situation more traumatic than it already was. My primary response to those that suggested involving the police was to protect my mom from any cruelty. She hadn't been the one to make this story national news!

The essay is one of the least formally inventive pieces I've published. The *NYT* is a news outlet. They publish what they call objective journalism. That doesn't mean I didn't use craft techniques and writing strategies. By including my mom and my daughter in the essay, I showed that the problem with the ruling spans generations. By writing about my daughter's college plans, I showed that I have gone on to have a relatively normal life, even after the potentially devastating effects of being molested and the shame that the anti-choice people tried to attach to abortion. I also slowed down the story enough to build scenes so I could transport my readers into the time and space. I described the first act of the molestation to ask readers to visualize the horror. I included another scene about the abortion to make readers imagine what might have happened if abortion had been illegal—which it would become in many states in the next year. I included a scene of me writing the essay on my computer—when my husband walked by, I closed the laptop. This scene showed that however much I had processed the trauma, I still felt shame. But, that shame? The minute I published the essay, it disappeared. The best effect, besides the number of emails and comments that thanked me for sharing my story, was that once I put the facts squarely out there, when I shaped the story myself, I felt transformed to someone this had happened to into someone who was going to do something with my story.

I don't want to go beyond my own experience to promote writing as therapeutic, but I will explain how writing and publishing have helped me shape my own story and taught me to move past shame. In the big metaphor between how I found love and support after my molestation and how trees and fungi support health forest growth, I can control, or at least name, the mushrooms that emerge from the mycorrhizal system that replaced my nervous system. Because I can write it, I can feather the story into the rest of my life. The story doesn't explain me; I explain my story. There's agency in that. Driving the sentences means that I'm driving the car. I take responsibility—not the kind that says, "oh it was all my fault," but the kind that says, "I determine the meaning of what happened to me." With enough skill and craft and work and art, I shape what my story means to readers. My mom, who has been with me through the whole of my story, is starting to write about her own story. She is shaping the facts, so she feels she's the subject, not the direct object, of the sentence, the topic sentence of the paragraph, the driver of the car.

"The act of telling itself changes the tale," Dr. van der Kolk writes in *The Body Keeps the Score*. To me, the fact that telling stories that are bent, crooked, sideways isn't a flaw in our culture but a corrective. Sometimes the dreck must be told even if it feels shitty to do it. Sometimes, the culture must listen to the dreck if it's going to become self-sustaining. Van Der Kolk concurs, in a way: "The mind cannot help but make meaning out of what it knows, and the meaning we make of our lives changes how and what we remember" (193).[2] Each story forms its own potential meaning. It is its own bit of mycelia that, unfurled, reaches out toward something hungry—meaning, a reader, understanding, a little tree-root, looking for something only the fungi can give it—selenium, perhaps.

In *How to Plant a Billion Trees,* one of the underlying premises is that healthy forests do a lot of work staving off climate change. Although I write a lot about personal troubles, environmental devastation dominates a lot of my work. Climate change seems as intractable a problem as sex abuse, abortion rights, and bodily autonomy. I want to puzzle out the problems in my mind—not necessarily because I will, as I weave between the threads of the problems, find the one right answer, but that as I write, I see one possible solution that may solve part of the problem. Or, more concisely, I see new ways to think about the problem. Donna Haraway in her book *Staying with the Trouble: Making Kin in the Chthulucene* (2016) argues that to stave off the worst effects of climate change, we who are acculturated in teleological philosophies will have to change the way we think.

To change the way we think will require changing the way we narrate our lives. Simple straightforward narratives don't always provide the catharsis we may desire. Haraway's version of staying with the trouble requires "learning to be truly present, not as a vanishing pivot between awful or Edenic pasts and apocalyptic or salvific futures but as mortal critters entwined in myriad unfinished configurations of places, times, matters, meanings." To stay with the trouble means to consider, even perform, different story lines. To stay with the trouble is to imagine different turning points as not *the* turning point, the line in the sand that you cross and from which you can never turn back. Staying with the trouble means keep turning back. Look at this story again. See what else there is. By pulling together two vastly separate storylines, I spend a lot of time seeing where the threads go. I make connections that I wouldn't if I didn't stay inside the trouble.

Many of the writing strategies I talk about in this book use metaphor, which, as must be obvious by now, is my favorite thing. You can see in the preceding paragraphs where I've relied on metaphor to explain what I'm getting at. The mycorrhizal fungal system is on my mind because that's what my latest book is about.

As we learn more about forest ecosystems, we begin to discover that even the chemical reactions like the ones that spur exchanges between mycorrhizal fungi and bacteria exist within the sapwood of the trees themselves. Researchers at the university where I work have visited the CZU Lightning Complex fire scar in Big Basin State Park in California that burned from August 19, 2020 to January 5, 2021. Thousands of acres of thousand-year-old trees that once stretched their green spires far into the atmosphere became ghost woods—ships transporting the dead from this green earth across the River Styx, which is also charred and full of ash. But their research shows that even dead-looking redwoods can sprout baby redwoods from the resources of their deep carbon stores. Up the ladder of these now "limb-less posts," a fuzzy carpet of green sprouts climbs 200 feet up those posts. These sprouts, looking as ambitious as asparagus in spring, grew using carbon the trees had absorbed and stored over 100 years ago. The researchers covered the buds with black plastic so the sun couldn't reach them, preventing any present-day photosynthesis. The research showed that the trees hadn't resprouted from present-day carbon dioxide in the atmosphere. Instead, the sprouts dug into sapwood to convert old-timey carbon the coastal redwoods had eaten years ago into new growth.

As my friend, George Koch, Professor of Ecosystem Science, said in an interview filmed by Erik about the research results, "the study is about understanding better the details really at the chemical level almost of how these trees are able to come back to rebuild a crown of vigorous green foliage after losing everything." If only I had George Koch's research savvy as I looked into the wilderness or into the wasteland of a future that seemed like it would ever be twisted by the babysitter. What if he had been there to explain that maybe what appears to be an entire devastation isn't necessarily so. Inside the tree, substances act. Seemingly invisible chemicals can spawn new growth.

In the metaphor of forest burning, the molestation and the subsequent abortion were the fire. The extreme event that destroyed so much of the terrain came from how old I was, from people knowing what happened, from shame and complicity. In a version of the story, the abortion—according to the forced-birthers, as an evil or a sin—caused the fire to burn more acreage, destroy even the canopy of trees: more shame, more loss, more ravaged sense of self. But, in fact, the abortion was the next batch of trees sprouting. If my mom hadn't called the Women's Clinic, if the babysitter's parents hadn't contributed $300 to the $600 cost, if abortion had been illegal not only in Utah but the United States, what would have happened to me? Now that I'm 100 years old, I can imagine that life, almost. If I had survived giving birth at age eleven, I would have either given the baby up for adoption or my parents would have helped me raise the child. My body would have endured the anachronistic maternity reshaping. I probably wouldn't have gone to Reed College. Maybe I wouldn't have gone to college at all. I would have had a hard time devoting myself to graduate school, if I got there. I probably wouldn't be a professor. I wouldn't live in the middle of the largest contiguous ponderosa pine forest in the lower 48. I wouldn't have my kids, Max and Zoë. I'd have a different kid who would be 41 to my 52.

My metaphor is imperfect. I struggled with equating molestation with the forest of my youth burning down because the forest also stands for the community into which I, if I was going to stave off the worst effects of molestation, needed to be enveloped. Can the metaphor shift?

The end of the book ends with a scene of me and my husband campaigning for him for Flagstaff Unified School Board, as well as for Katie Hobbs, our would-be governor, and Kathy Hoffman, who lost to Tom Horne, voucher magnate, book banner, and public-school eviscerator, as State School Superintendent. As we walked around town, we discovered neighborhoods we'd never visited. As I canvassed, I imagined hyphae, those hairs of the underground fungi, spooling out behind me. These hairs connected neighbor to neighbor. I was connected via sidewalk from house to house, would-be voter to would-be voter. If one could pace every sidewalk in Flagstaff, would that knit our community closer together? In the world of metaphor, can you use the word "knit," when you're talking about mushrooms and mycorrhizal fungi? I take the liberty because scientific texts use the word thread and thread is close enough, I hope, to yearn for the mind to associatively grow, to sew a fabric.

Metaphor pulls things together. Hooks that stitch. But I know that the extended metaphor stretches awfully far. I know it is a risk to talk about this fungal system that lives underground as if it's obviously the sign for how humans build community. It's an imperfect art. Maybe even artifice, but my ethic behind it is this: If we can imagine connective links between hummingbirds and nervous foot-thrumming, between eggs and creativity, between rabbits and Poprocks, we can see ourselves in the world around us, and—if we're really good at this game—in each other.

A metaphor, in official literary theory terms, contains a vehicle and a tenor. The tenor is the thing being described. The vehicle is the figurative language that *moves* the reader to an emotive reaction, to a greater understanding, or a new way of seeing the subject. As you may have noticed, my metaphors flip vehicles and tenors back and forth and upside down. This is probably, theoretically, inadvisable. Readers like to know where they're going. Someone should drive the car. But one of the benefits of playing fast and loose with vehicle and tenor is that you can stretch the content to its limit. The more stuff there is to work with, the more stuff one can make. In order to complicate the metaphor, you have to research all aspects of your vehicle. The more tenors you have, the more possibilities you have for vehicle. And, conversely, the more intensely you describe the details of your story, the more primary subject you can connect your metaphors to.

My professor at Utah, the poet Donald Revell, cautioned against metaphor. Metaphor, by bringing together unlike things, risks occluding one of the objects, if not both of them. How can I see the lion if I call him king? If my nervous system is mycorrhizal fungi, then where did the nerve's ability to make a foot thrum go? Or, possibly worse: Why should this complex, forest-building system be relegated to a single human's description of her experience?

My solution to both the problem of occlusion and subjugation is to keep the metaphor moving. In some parts of *Billion Trees*, my interiority parallels the fungi. In other parts, it's the whole forest that has burned down. In other parts, it's the work of rebuilding connections, as mycelia do, that one must undertake to stitch oneself back into a community, back into a life from which they felt cut off.

With much metaphor comes much responsibility. When I was younger, I didn't use the words "sexual assault" or "rape" or "molestation" because I wanted to acknowledge that I didn't say no. That I let the babysitter have sex with me more than once. That I created soap opera-like fantasies so I could handle the molestation. Once I acknowledged that I hadn't been responsible for what happened to me as a kid, I started taking responsibility in a different way. Part of it was thanks to the *NYT* piece that stated what happened in non-metaphor detail with a purpose. I wanted people to know the doom the Dobb's decision would cause. I also took responsibility by trying to shape my story into something that went beyond the narrative of one little girl who ran into some trouble and, with a billion ropes of rescue, managed to make an OK life for herself. I want to be responsible with the metaphor. To let it breathe and move so my story doesn't occlude the magical systems at work in the natural world. And, I wanted the story to be as complicated as that shifting metaphor—to show that harm to others permeates and spreads and burns and cleaves, and that others can knit the fractures, can stem the landslide, can hose down the burns with their patience and willingness to see that sullied person, that ruined landscape differently.

Notes

1 Colin Miazga, Paul Bauman, Alastair McClymont, and Chris Slater (2021), "Geophysical investigation of the Miła 18 resistance bunker in Warsaw, Poland," *SEG Technical Program Expanded Abstracts*: 3096–3100. https://doi.org/10.1190/segam2021-3594939.1.
2 Bessel van der Klerk, *The Body Keeps the Score,* Viking (1996).

Chapter 3

WHY RESEARCH?

In a story I wrote about my mother growing up very poor in an isolated town in Wyoming, I compared her childhood to this special kind of sand that exists only in a few places on earth—the Bahamas, the Mediterranean Sea, and the Great Salt Lake. Most sand is usually ground-down mountains and seashells. This sand is built up: a tiny pellet of brine shrimp waste or a small fleck of shell, as it swings back and forth in salty waves, is coated by layers of calcium carbonate. Because of the swinging, the salt, and the addition of more layers of calcium carbonate, this sand is shaped uniquely into what is called Oolite. Ooli means egg-like. In the essay, I move back and forth between my mom finding a way out of poverty and details about how this sand grows itself. In the end, I show how my mom is like the Oolitic soil—by making hard choices about her family, reading books, she rejects her ancestral destiny to be poor and subject to men's whims to become someone in charge of her own existence. She built her life up from tiny fecal pellet to a special, beautiful egg-shaped grain of sand. The form of the essay, this back-and-forth, echoes the content of the essay, but I cannot say I knew exactly where I was going when I thought "mom!" and "fancy sand of the Great Salt Lake."

It's thanks to researching the fancy sand that I started to pull these ideas together. I know my mom's story pretty well. She was born to a father who had a drinking and robbery problem and a mother who had a fertility problem. Too much fertility, not too little. My grandma's mother was even more abundantly fertile. My Mormon great-grandmother had eight kids by an abusive Mormon man. Evanston, Wyoming, is the kind of town whose size seemed to squeeze the meanness out of people. My mom escaped that. Eventually. I knew my mom's story, but I knew very little about how Oolitic sand worked. Through researching the sand, I saw the aim of the essay: Although my mom could have been eroded and ground down by a familial, religious heritage, she escaped instead. She left that corrosive system for a life that she built up, tiny calcium carbonate layer by tiny calcium carbonate layer.

By learning about Oolitic sand, I saw my mom's story in a new light. As I toggled between paragraphs about her and paragraphs about calcium carbonate, mother-of-pearl, aragonite, Appalachia, and actual pearls, the "meaning" of the story became clear. My mother had done something special in ways I hadn't understood or formulated before.

Research is not only useful for making metaphors, but also for making the other kind of hard stuff—not so much the personal, or the personally political—make sense to readers in a personal way. I'm not a reporter. Even when I try to be objective, I use the first-person to apologize for not knowing everything I should know. I wanted to write an essay about how climate change is the driver for so many of our current wars, but I couldn't make myself do it. It wasn't the research that I dreaded. I wanted to know if I was right. The problem was the declarative statement. To assert that "climate change is the primary driver for the war in Gaza, the Ukraine, or Congo," I would have to ignore all the other potential reasons for war—and, obviously, climate change is not the sole reason for any of these wars. Because I am unconvinced of the finality of any assertion, I have a hard time writing opinion pieces that don't waffle. And, as I dig into the research further, I realize there are plenty of reasons for waffling. The people of the Democratic Republic of Congo are suffering from drought and flooding caused by climate change more than those in the Global North—but they're also suffering from years of colonialism, authoritarianism, resource extraction, seemingly constant war, and ethnic cleansing. After the Rwandan genocide in 1994, when Hutu extremists killed an estimated 800,000 minority ethnic Tutsis and moderate Hutus in Rwanda (DRC's neighbor to the east), nearly two million Hutu refugees poured into Congo. Tutsi militants retaliated. Congo's Tutsis, with Rwandan backing, attacked Zaire, where Mobuto Sese Seko ruled cruelly. The cruelty intensified from all directions as power flip-flopped from one extremist group to another.

My argument that climate change is a factor seems secondary to post-colonial power grabs. It seems tertiary to the violent extraction of humans and their resources by the colonialists. Sometimes, research talks us out of an essay, which in this case, was the right thing. While the marriage between my mother and Oolitic soil began as a happy coincidence, it became a tool for drilling deeper into both sides of the story. In the too-huge-for-me-at-least topic of war and climate change, the tool that began as a drill became a shovel, then a spoon, then not even a thimble.

David Carlin, my friend and co-author of *The After-Normal: Brief, Alphabetical Essays on a Changing Planet* connects personal narrative to larger events like climate change. His writing is sharp, insightful, smart, and, if this is a word one might use for writing, kind. He bestows upon his subject thoughtfulness and admiration. Whether it is for a circus performer who emigrated from Ethiopia to Melbourne or to "Plasmodia," one of the essays in our co-written collection, David builds his words up from the essence of his material, similar to Oolitic soil's process. Instead of harnessing or capturing a topic, he follows the arc and motion of his subjects. It's an ethic that preserves the integrity of that subject and one that lets the reader have an open response to the subject.

David writes the big stuff. From climate change to immigration and colonialism, his capacious mind can wrap around global topics, but he enters them through the incisive detail. In the essay, "Grief" from *The After-Normal*, he describes the loss he feels as he contemplates a dead penguin that has washed up on the beach, couching it in the sense of loss we feel for all that's disappearing because of the climate crisis: ice shelves, forests, shorelines.

David uses research and metaphor to puncture assumptions about the rarity of lyrebirds. Lyrebirds, if you don't know, are master mimickers. They can sound like a camera click, a monkey's howl, or a man laughing. In an essay about them, published in an essay called "Lyrebirds in the Impasse," as part of the *Bending Genre* anthology I edited with Margot Singer, David describes the lyrebird as he happens upon one, and then another, on a long walk:

> A lyrebird surprised me. It was almost within reach, on a raised ledge to one side of the path. I stopped to watch it. It had no interest in me, or fear. Humans who walk these paths must pose no threat to lyrebirds, or so it seemed to believe. It was busy scratching at the soft, thick bed of forest leaves, digging beneath for the sweet and succulent worms to be found there, stooping its head every now and then to gobble one. Its long tail feathers swung in the darkening air behind it.
>
> The lyrebird went about its victuals with an observable grace and dignity. It was both sovereign and subject. It knew things I would never know. It lived a life I could not imagine. But it was as if, just by its presence, it was holding me to account.
>
> (66)[1]

David describes the bird's actions and movements. He doesn't quite veer into anthropomorphizing it, but recognizes within it an "observable grace and dignity." Staring at the lyrebird, spending time observing its eating practice, its stature, its tail feathers, give this bird the time it deserves to be perfectly its own creature. It is only after such objective description does Carlin allow himself to wonder what the bird could know. Such wondering leads him to consider how long will lyrebirds remain extant in this changing climate?

> In how many short years of scudding clouds met by an increasingly impatient sun will this valley no longer accommodate lyrebirds, because of some subtle amendment of the food chain or unsubtle black earth annihilation: a fire storm racing up from below as if from a fissure in the Earth's crust? Incineration, plague, starvation—?
>
> (66)[2]

The idea that the lyrebird holds Carlin's narrator to account is to change the agency of the subject. The subject makes an impact upon the narrator that, thanks to the narrator's close concern, only that narrator can perceive. From here, he takes this moment as an impasse: a detente between observer and bird. From there, Carlin leaps into other moments of impasse. As the essay describes the kinds of impasses the narrator encounters: stuck in writer's block, stopped at one, then two, then three extravagantly gorgeous places near his home in Melbourne, Australia, restrained by depressions, halted by indecision, Carlin turns the idea of impasse on its head.

Perhaps the stopping isn't the problem. Perhaps it's the point. Echoes of Haraway's "staying with the trouble" resonate throughout the idea of "impasse." Carlin refers to Maggie Nelson, author of *The Argonauts* and coiner of the term "auto-criticism," as she notes that writing is always about a body in time. I often tell my creative writing students to put your body in a place. All readers, just as lyrebirds, have bodies. If you put yourself, your characters, your narrators, in a place, the reader's body will follow along with yours. If I add "time" to that 'body in place' advice, I approach what Carlin's finally realizes about how being at an impasse can twist whatever presumptions we'd been working with into something new and surprising. Lyrebirds are not endangered but you have to travel to where they live. The danger here comes from the concern that "where they live" is under threat—because so many places are. Over the course of the essay, Carlin has seen four, which is a lot for a single walk. He notes in the last lines of the piece: "The lyrebirds and I composed our scenes together, those moments we stopped each other in our tracks, and whatever we were repeating, were also changing, turning sideways."

Carlin's research isn't overtly perceptible. He writes with authority about the lyrebirds as well as Queen Elizabeth II stopping to take in the view of Jamison Bay while drawing upon the irreality of *The Truman Show*. He cites other writers whose work also considers temporality, like Lauren Berlant, Paul Theroux, and Maggie Nelson, who layer support for the discourse on how stopping in one's tracks can lead to a new start. The lyrebirds aren't the metaphor. They're the reason David had to stop and rejig his relationship to the impasse. Without the impasse, the essay and its textured perceptions wouldn't exist.

To layer metaphor and research together, it helps to read a lot. I listened to the audiobook version of Viet Thanh Nguyen's *The Sympathizer*. Audiobooks are great for multitasking; I listen to a book a week while I walk or run my dogs, Bear and Zora. But audiobooks are not so helpful for bookmarking specific craft choices I notice an author making. Still, Nguyen's novel is so replete with metaphors that I could Google the ones I remembered. The lines I read were delivered to me with a little help from AI as I typed the words "Campbell Soup" and Viet Thanh Nguyen's name into ChatGPT's search field.

In my nonfiction books, like Nguyen, I rely on leitmotif, extended metaphor, recurring images, and repeated phrasing help give a text texture and cohesion. I love the Easter eggs of repeated words. Like notes combined to make a chord, they resonate. Sometimes, reading *The Sympathizer* I laughed out loud at his recurrences. He references Campbell Soup more than Andy Warhol. Even though *The Sympathizer* is a book about a hard thing—escaping Vietnam as the US pulled out, trying to make it as an immigrant in Los Angeles, murder, working with Hollywood to "adapt" the war to the screen, Nguyen uses these recurring metaphors, as well as humor, to add a contemporary perspective to a conflict that has been rendered repeatedly by book and screen, which I'll discuss more deeply in the chapter on metaphor.

Metaphors make space. They make space for humor. They make space for meaning. They open entry ways for readers who might just be in love with lyrebirds or are fascinated with the post-modern cant and camp of the use of Campbell Soup in Nguyen's *Sympathizer*. Metaphors also help us remember when hard stuff takes over our concentration. In Sarah Manguso's *Ongoingness: The End of a Diary*, she writes about the kind of attention one pays through writing a diary: jotted observations, logs, lists, secret loves, and desires. But when one shapes that diary into something readable, the process of remembering goes meta. The book centers around the birth of her son and what happens to her memory when she's pregnant and postpartum. She writes about writing—and how "things" that once helped her to recover her memory were failing her:

> It used to be that things always reminded me of a lot of other things.
>
> Then, for eighteen months or so, they didn't. In the diary I recorded only facts. Minutes of nursing, ounces of milk, hours of sleep.
>
> Things were just themselves. I was too exhausted or hormone-drunk or depressed to think of anything that resembled anything else.
>
> That's how things appear to an infant.
>
> (67)[3]

In lieu of metaphor, or even objects to organize her thinking, Manguso uses white space like a poem might use stanza breaks. You need space to make metaphors and her postpartum brain had no space except for the immediate surroundings of her and her infant. As Manguso struggles to log her existence, the way she made space was literally by hitting the "enter" key on her computer twice. In between the lines is where meaning is made.

Many lyric essays work through white space and short vignettes. The tension between the vignettes not only gives the writer space to handle the hard stuff, but the white space also makes an entry point for the reader to come in and make meaning. Steve Fellner's most recent collection, *Eating Lightbulbs and Other Essays*, invokes some seriously hard stuff: bipolar disorder, a father's homelessness, a mother's cancer and ensuing dementia. But in an essay as meta-narrative as Manguso, *On Fragmentation*, Fellner wonders what the effect of these tiny, assertive segments of an essay amounts to:

> Once I developed a severe case of urticaria. I can still remember the ER nurse surveying the red splotches all over my skin. I asked her if I should be worried. "You're still breathing. That's always a good thing," she said. That's when I knew I was in trouble. What was weird about these hives was that they would move. You'd see a rash on my upper neck; if you closed your eyes for a second, they'd disappear and show up somewhere else: my neck, arm, or even forehead. They wouldn't stop moving. You couldn't trace a definite trajectory—the appearance of the hives seemed almost arbitrary. After I accepted the fact that this urticaria was going to continue indefinitely, my relation to Time

became different. I couldn't pinpoint the moment when something revealed itself and then when it vanished. Everything was blurry and fragmented.

*

I never trust people who love Sappho. It seems cowardly. It's always easy to say that you like something based on a few fragments. Or maybe I'm the coward. I always want to fill in the blanks with unambiguous solutions. I always believe that if you look hard enough, you can find something else that you see as definite, essential.

*

Four years ago, I had a nervous breakdown, culminating in a diagnosis of bipolar disorder. What bothered me the most was sleeplessness. Before I received the proper diagnosis, it turned out I was wrongly diagnosed and given an anti-depressant, jettisoning me into mania.

I didn't fall asleep for three days. I lost track of time. Wakefulness never seemed to end. I needed to experience time in smaller stretches. Little fragments of eternity.

*

When I grade freshmen composition essays, I sense that I always become more annoyed when I spot a sentence fragment as opposed to a run-on sentence. How American is it to assume that more is more?

*

When I was manic, I couldn't sit down. I didn't know what got into me. I didn't know how I was going to continue at the rate I was going. I thought I was going to die. I decided that if I was going to die I had to write my mother a love letter.

The best way I knew how to write someone a love letter was to write a book.
    How to begin?

> I sat down at the computer and typed a single quotation my mother had once said to me.
>
> I had been excessively apologizing to people for things I didn't have any control over.
>
> She slapped me and said: "Don't live your life like a woman. Don't live your life as an apology."
>
> I read my mother the quotation. "I said that?" she said, "That's pretty damn good."
>
> "That's part of a new book I'm writing," I said, "It's the first sentence."
>
> "Whatever happened to Once Upon a Time?"
>
> (191–2)[4]

Feller moves between a skin disease, Sappho, mental health, the narrator's mother, sentences, and a manic episode in two pages. The essay becomes braided by the end, where we see where the connection between mental stress and writing comes together, but the first few segments seem independent from each other. This has two effects: one is that the writer casts a wide net to harness a big idea. The other is that it creates a distance from the material to stave off whatever self-indulgence might lie in describing one's mental health. The essay culminates in an exegesis about what fragmentation in writing can do:

> A memoir-in-fragments confesses the disposability of literature. Let's face it: there's always something you can cut out that no one will notice. And if they do notice: they'll just assume it's in the white space, begging for their attention.

*

> When I first started sending my mother fragments she said, "What are you going to do with all these things?"
>
> "I don't know," I said. "Maybe I'll keep them the way they are."
>
> She said, "That's crazy. Everyone will think you've written a book of poetry."
>
> "Maybe I have," I said.

"Oh no!" she said, "No one reads poetry. How am I supposed to become famous?
 Respect your mother. Turn me into prose. You owe me that."

*

When you're writing an essay-in-fragments, should each fragment be a complete thing in and of itself? Or does it need to transcend itself, existing for something larger? Should we even think of transcendence as a goal in literature? Should the goal simply be to allow?

*

I wrote an essay-in-fragments for a creative writing teacher. During the workshop, he said: Kill all your darlings.

I raised my hand and asked, "Can you be a little more specific. They're all my darlings."

(120–1)

Like Nguyen's metaphors, the space Fellner opens between anecdotes creates space for humor. Humor requires that shift from expected to unexpected, from real to surreal in short strokes. These segments allow for those quick turns. White space between the fragments creates distance between the narrator and the author, the narrator and the reader. They also create a character of a mother, written in fragments, who wants to be written in prose. Fellner argues both sides of an argument. Can fragmentation approach a whole perspective? And, is all writing, sentence by sentence, a collection of fragments? One nice thing about opening white space between statements, ideas, and scenes is that you have enough room to turn and show how both notions that "fragments are disruptive" and "fragments are essential" can exist at the same time.

It's amazing what our brains can do. They can create a narrative where there isn't one. They can fill in the blanks while they simultaneously revel in the beauty of the fragment. Writing that jumps, implies connections that aren't explicitly made, that uses associations more than transitions to link paragraphs, is called parataxis. Parataxis is a writing technique that involves placing independent clauses one after another without using conjunctions to connect them. It can create a sense of urgency and immediacy and can make writing sound more spoken. "I came, I saw, I conquered" is an example of parataxis. The counter-mode is hypotaxis, a grammatical technique that involves using connecting words to show the relationship between clauses or sentences. This technique can help readers analyze the relationships between clauses and can highlight the importance of certain clauses. "I am tired because it is hot" is an example of hypotaxis.

In parataxis, the sentences, clauses, and phrases are not coordinated or subordinated. Similar to the braided essay I discussed in my own writing, the paratactic collects multiple ideas and structures them horizontally, associatively. Perhaps we can look to the grammar of Gerard Manley Hopkins. Hopkins, a Jesuit priest who subversively finds God in the grounded world of flora and fauna, wrote paratactically. With capitalized "ANDs" and lists of verbs and nouns to trace a hawk, Hopkins' syntax makes an even playing field for a world imbued by God. Instead of spiritual structure where God rules humans and humans rule the beasts, Hopkins' poetry radiates immanence, the belief that God exists inside everything. This is no longer a vertical spirituality but a horizontal one. If writing can make real change, I believe it happens at basic levels, like syntax and grammar. As we've come to understand how important a person's pronouns can be to one's identity, those of us who want to affirm another's sense of self, work hard to perfect our speech. As we think about the difference between "lay" and "lie," and curse ourselves for forgetting which is which, we wonder about whether our bodies are a subject or an object. "I lie down, but I lay my body upon the bed." As we work through these grammatical tics, we rearrange our understanding of subject and object, pronoun and noun. Hopkins does this with parataxis. Hopkins' reshuffling of where the Windhover flies—across the sky with God, perhaps even as a part of God—he imagines a different kind of spirituality where everyone has equal access to God and is equal to God. In Hopkins' poem, *The Windhover, To Christ Our Lord*, a kestrel travels up and down, knitting the sky to the earth. In the very middle of the poem, the bird holds its own against the wind, which moves the speaker's heart.

> Rebuffed the big wind. My heart in hiding
> Stirred for a bird, – the achieve of, the mastery of the thing!

That dash is paratactic, serving as an equal sign. And the bird pulls air and his feathers together. The buckle is both break and connect, both fracture and splint. The bird is both speaker and character, both bird and knight, flight and God.

Brute beauty and valour and act, oh, air, pride, plume, here
Buckle! AND the fire that breaks from thee then, a billion
Times told lovelier, more dangerous, O my chevalier!

The falcon is of the sky and the ground. He's on fire. He *is* fire. He is lovely. He is dangerous. He's valorous and bestial. He contains multitudes. He is agent of his own definition. He is action. Donna Haraway writes "multispecies storytelling" that is "about recuperation in complex histories that are as full of dying as of living, as full of endings, even genocides, as beginnings . . . real stories that are also speculative fabulations and speculative realisms." (Haraway, *Staying with the Trouble*.) As I write about in *How to Plant a Billion Trees*, as I make the connection between human healing and forest health, I argue that if we are to imagine a world where humans and their environment aren't set against each other, if the planet isn't merely resources to extract, if the humans begin to understand their collective connection to the planet, we must be able to imagine the agency of others—perhaps the most radical agency to imagine is that of animals themselves, like Hopkins' falcon.

When making connections, or when using the image of a web or network as a metaphor for how writing the hard stuff can work, imagining objects and subjects on an even playing field lets the metaphor work. Webs grow horizontally, vertically, and across. As we readers stretch their minds following our leaps and falls, meaning spins into place.

Parataxis works through creating enough space between subjects for associations to happen. When writing the hard stuff, you also need space between you and your subject to make your own energetic meaning. In my nonfiction classes, I even ask my students to call themselves "narrator" when talking about themselves on the page to wedge that distance into the workshop and into the writers. Metaphors can create space to provide distance that you might need—especially if you don't have time to create distance. Sometimes, like I had to with the *NYT* piece, you have to write the hard stuff right now. Sometimes, writing that hard stuff immediately can come off as flat. Opening up the story by using metaphor, objects, braids, and white space can give it the dimension the story deserves.

I recently taught a class for students in a National Science Foundation-supported program called PROCESS. The intent of the class was to connect creative experience with scientific thought, deepening the student's investment in both in the process. In the morning, the students collected microorganisms from soil samples. In the afternoon, I, along with a master's student in biology, Megan Quinn, in our MFA program's Environmental Narrative Certificate, taught them about fundamentals of creative writing while my colleague, Neal Galloway, taught them about art and earth works.

Writing about science is hard. Writing about science *creatively* is extra hard. Figuring out how to write about big, complicated topics through specific strategies, weaponized differently in different genres is hard, but it stretches your imagination, letting you exercise your brain as you experiment. During a class Megan organized around the idea of story, she turned the mic over to me to discuss core concepts like plot, character, theme, point of view, and conflict, climax, resolution. We read Paolo Bacigalupi's short story *The Tamarisk Hunter*, Robin Wall Kimmerer's essay "The Teaching of Grasses", Linda Hogan's poem "Innocence", and a scientific article, "Not just about the trees: Key role of mosaic-meadows in restoration of ponderosa pine ecosystem" by Megan Shanahan Matonis and Dan Binkley. It's one thing to apply those core concepts of plot, character, theme, point of view, and conflict, climax, resolution to fiction, but it's particularly fun to apply these core concepts to essays, poems, and science articles because the terms don't so easily fit.

We mapped out conflict in each of the texts. For *The Tamarisk Hunter*, the conflict centers around Lolo, the main character, who is paid to remove tamarisk trees that, individually, as the story begins, "can suck 73,000 gallons of river water a year. For $2.88 a day, plus water bounty, Lolo rips tamarisk all winter long." However, in a decades-long drought along the Colorado River, Lolo plants seeds while he pulls the plants, in order to insure a long tamarisk-pulling career. Conflicted indeed!

In Kimmerer's "The Teaching of Grasses", we found that the conflict roiled between systems of knowledge. On the one hand, scientists in the academic community claimed that harvesting native grasses denuded the meadows. But, informed by Lena, an elder in the tribe who volunteered traditional Ways of Knowing, Kimmerer's student Laurie found that harvesting grasses actually resulted in an abundance of new grass. Traditional ways of knowing run directly against academic ways of knowing, creating conflict.

The students struggled a bit with the poem but once we stuck with it for a while, we uncovered some of the ways Linda Hogan's poem moved.

Innocence

There is nothing more innocent
than the still-unformed creature I find beneath soil,

neither of us knowing what it will become
in the abundance of the planet.
It makes a living only by remaining still
in its niche.
One day it may struggle out of its tender
pearl of blind skin
with a wing or with vision
leaving behind the transparent.

I cover it again, keep laboring,
hands in earth, myself a singular body.
Watching things grow,
wondering how
a cut blade of grass knows
how to turn sharp again at the end.

This same growing must be myself,
not aware yet of what I will become
in my own fullness
inside this simple flesh.⁵

We started by looking at the repeated sounds at the ends of the lines. In the first stanza, innocent's "t" is recalled by the "t" at the end of planet and of transparent, the "l"s recur in soil and still, and the near rhyme of skin and vision. Listen to all the "f" sounds in the third stanza, I offered. One reason to draw out the consonance and assonance, aside from the sheer delight of finding these sonic repetitions, is that it forces the reader to stay a little longer in the poem. The professor who led the science portion of process said, "I never really liked poetry but I'm starting to see how fun it can be."

"The poem itself is a metaphor for the work you're doing," I suggested. As you go into the field, discover microorganisms, bring them back to the lab, and study them under the microscope, you're doing what Logan does in the poem: going into the dirt to look at something very closely "to find beneath the soil . . . what it will become in the abundance of the planet,'" I went on. The possibilities abound. And, as the poem says, the poem does just that: It suggests that poetry is something that, like a microorganism under the scope, under close study, reveals abundance that defines innocence anew. Innocence doesn't mean "unsullied" or "untouched." In fact, it's seeded in dirt. The word "Innocence" is newly defined as the moment of attention on the verge of becoming anything.

We even applied core concepts to the scientific paper finding the conflict in the hypothesis: mosaic meadows support ponderosa pine forests. Refuting previous policy where foresters replant only trees after a devastating fire, this study showed that "The long-term sustainability of ponderosa pine ecosystems may depend on mosaic-meadows that provide fine fuels and support frequent, low-severity fires." As the students and I mapped core concepts onto this array of diverse genres, we began to understand that we had to define the terms within the context of their writing. We saw that character develops within the story, through the setting, dialogue, scene, and plot. Then, as we discussed point of view and theme, we saw they too emerged distinctly within their genre and within their purpose or message. One student, Peter, noticed, "Community structures are important for community growth so when you plant a tree farm in a meadow, you take away that community support." Then, I noted that key concepts interplay in texts to make the story they're trying to tell. Neither conflict nor character nor plot nor point of view exist without the support of each other. Once again, the subject of the story paralleled the insights into craft we'd garnered, as we made form follow content on the fly.

By taking four different genres, four different points of view, different assemblages of character, and different plot lines to describe core contexts, we could see that each text had its own point of view and its own voice. Although one may be able to discern some similarity in the voices across the literary texts, the distinct voice of each of these pieces rang unique. We wondered whether the scientific article had a voice. Scientific papers are supposed to be objective, and therefore, without a personal voice. But this particular scientific paper was written with such strong verbs, such descriptive settings, that even though the "we" in the paper wasn't knowable as either Megan Shanahan Matonis or Dan Binkley, the paper not only announced a "scientific paper voice," it announced a descriptive and accessible, even singular, one.

Kimmerer's voice in her essay is not singular. She uses the form of a scientific paper with the well-known sections of Introduction, Literature Review, Hypothesis, Methods, Results, Discussion, Conclusion, Acknowledgements, and References Cited. References Cited includes not your standard "Scientist et. al" references but instead, *Wiingaashk*, Buffalo, Lena, the Ancestors.

> As her baby grew, Laurie came to believe with increasing conviction in the knowledge of her basket-making mentors, recognizing, as Western science often does not, the quality of observations from the

home who had long had close relationships with plants and their habitats. They shared many of their teachings with her, and they knit many baby hats.

Baby Celia was born in the early fall, and a braid of sweetgrass was hung over her crib. While Celia slept nearby, Laurie put her data on the computer and began to make the comparisons between the harvesting methods. From the twist ties on every stem, Laurie could chart the births and deaths in the sample plots. Some plots were full of new young shoots that signaled a thriving population, and some were not. Her statistical analyses were all sound and thorough, but she hardly needed graphs to tell the story. From across the field you could see the difference: some plots gleamed shiny golden green, and some were dull and brown. The committee's criticism hovered in her mind: "Anyone knows that harvesting a plant will damage the population."

The surprise was that the failing plots were not the harvested ones, as predicted, but the unharvested controls. The sweetgrass that had not been picked or disturbed in any way was choked with dead stems while the harvested plots were thriving. Even though half of all stems had been harvested each year, they quickly grew back, completely replacing everything that had been gather, in fact producing more shoots than were present before harvest. Picking sweetgrass seemed to actually stimulate growth.

(162)[6]

In what creative nonfiction scholar Brenda Miller would call a "hermit-crab essay," Kimmerer played on the tropes of scientific papers, emptying out as if a shell. Then, she inserted her own content into that shell, upending the formal conceits of a scientific paper. The purpose of her essay is to demonstrate that traditional ways of knowing are as important and successful as scholarly, academic ways of knowing. This inversion of the scientific article's form contributes to the narrator's voice. The narrator sounds variously authoritative, lyrical, scientific, and, when talking about her student Laurie's baby and her ancestor Lena, her voice is as sweet as the grass Laurie picks in her experiment.

The concept of "voice" sounds monolithic, but voice can shift across the expanse of a book. In fact, it probably should. If the goal is to draw in as many readers to hear your story, offering multiple avenues to access the manuscript can come from an array of voices. As I worked with David Carlin of lyrebird fame on our book *The After-Normal*, we found that our voices differed from each other but, as we sent our brief, alphabetical essays back and forth, making the book an epistolary project, we responded to each other's choice of words or jokes, which sometimes aligned our voices. But in other essays, our take was so different that one of us saw the subject as serious, the other, funny. I learned that one's point of view, along with the depth of one's knowledge, shapes voice. I also learned that David's voice is so beautiful and strong, I had to work not to copy his erudition. My voice, although it shifts, begins at matter of fact and ends at sardonic. Our resulting book evoked many notes, different voices, a range of emotions as our brief, alphabetical essays resonated with each other.

Voice is tricky when writing the hard stuff. As we craft our sentences and choose our words, solemnity may dictate the tone. Depending on the weight of the hard stuff, an air of gravitas may pervade the style. Often, this is the best approach. Still, not all solemnity and gravity sound the same. My *NYT* essay was serious and straightforward. However, when I wrote *How to Plant a Billion Trees*, I could not sustain a solemn and grave tone throughout the whole book. Because I shift between kinds of texts and different modes, like shifting between a Robin Wall Kimmerer essay, a Hogan poem, science writing, and narrative, my voice shifts too. And, like Nguyen and Fellner, moving around, invoking metaphor, made room for humor too, even in this dark scene from *How to Plant a Billion Trees*.

> When I first suspected I was pregnant, I remember sitting on the toilet, looking at the white white white toilet paper. My copy of *Our Bodies Ourselves* opened automatically to the page about signs you are pregnant. I knew what white toilet paper meant. I pinched the skin where underneath my ovaries were supposed to be. "No, no, no," I told them. But it was too late. The ovaries weren't listening. I looked at my belly button. If I could tunnel in through there, maybe I could untie whatever knot had been tied. I could fly Superman around my uterus and undo.
>
> At some point, I got off the toilet and pulled my pants up. I punched my 11-year-old thigh. I thought shit, shit, shit since I hadn't learned how to say fuck yet. I thought of the number pi and the way cells divide. The numbers would just keep multiplying. This was out of my control. *This* being my body. *This* being. Body. It wasn't mine to do with anymore. I didn't tell my mom. I told the babysitter, as he sat at the piano in his parents' living room.
>
> "I think I'm pregnant," I said. In front of him, I didn't feel shame. Just perplexed and ready for a good plan. I don't think I thought he would ask to marry me, but maybe I did. My imagination whirled like

the VHS tapes where Superman kissed Lois Lane, or Luke kissed Leia, or on my soap opera, Luke kissed Laura on *General Hospital* although in retrospect all of those kisses were awkward and inappropriate. Luke had raped Laura and *then* they started dating. No wonder I had a skewed sense of what love was supposed to look like. I lived in a story of my own making—a parallel universe where I was older and we were properly dating and all of this was as normal as six-legged frogs, in this particular incarnation of our world. My imagination, if not my body, embraced its full autonomy. I was allowed to think anything I wanted.

I wanted the babysitter to walk up to me and tell me everything would be all right. I wanted different dialogue, different place, different time, different bodies. I had written this scene in my head. I'd tell him I was pregnant. He'd say, "Let's tell our parents together. We can get married. I know you have a favorite doll named Amber. Perhaps we can name the baby Amber." Instead, he yelled, "shit!" so loud I thought my mom across the street might hear him. But I didn't shush him. He went over to the stereo to put on ABBA's "Super Trouper" and stared out the window, saying "shit" a million times to himself under his breath. I wanted to sing along to the music. Maybe I did.

The first paragraph leans into lyricism with the repetition of the word white and the semi-fantastical image of tunneling through my belly button. The second paragraph is almost harsh. The anger I took out on my body, on myself, for allowing this to happen comes out in the italicized words and the short, hard sentences. The third paragraph turns to scene. Here, I try to relay the weird mental gymnastics my brain did to make the molestation not molestation but instead, a romantic story. Here and in the fourth paragraph, I let my imagination soothe my eleven-year-old mind. Kids at this age love to read and watch fantasy. I willed myself to live it. The fifth paragraph startles with the interjection. Here, I contrast what I fantasized with reality in the starkness of the swear word and the exclamation point. The final sentences about wanting to take refuge in unreality—wanting to just sing my troubles away—turns back to the lyricism of the first sentence, hoping that the wistful line nails the cognitive dissonance of the moment. The triply repeated "white" along with the triply repeated "no" feels uncomfortable to me. The weird imagery seems inharmonious, a superman flying around a uterus. The short sentences too seem jagged and harsh. This is a hard scene for me to recall. It's even hard for me to write about writing it, but I will do anything to make meaning out of pain. As I shift through voices here, I maintain that basic matter of fact tone, but use different elements of voice to convey the shifts in perspective.

Besides, "a foolish consistency is the hobgoblin of little minds," said Ralph Waldo Emerson. I want to write stories for big minds, and I want to read stories written by those with bigger minds than I have. I want to learn how people have turned their hard stuff into something palpable and meaningful. I want to laugh even though the story is so tough. I want to know all the voices on your pages. I want to see how our stories connect and how we can find ways to share them with others.

Notes

1. David Carlin, *Bending Genre*, Bloomsbury Publishing (2023).
2. Ibid.
3. Sarah Manguso, *Ongoingness: The End of a Diary*, Graywolf Press (2015).
4. Steve Fellner, "On Fragmentation," *Eating Lightbulbs and Other Essays*, Ohio State University Press (2021).
5. Linda Hogan, "Innocence," *Dark. Sweet,* Coffee House Press (2014).
6. Robin Kimmerer, "Mishkos Kenomagwen: The Teaching of Grasses," *Braiding Sweetgrass* (2013)

Chapter 4

WHAT HARD STUFF?

Let's face it. There is very little stuff to write about that *isn't* hard. Putting words on a page is hard enough. Now we're supposed to have a topic, a premise, a subject, a scene, image banks, characters, texture, dialogue, and lyric intensity? This book's dream is that writing hard stuff engenders craft. By putting pressure on a hard story, creativity burbles forth, like popping bubble wrap.

I've been writing hard stuff since I first started putting pen to paper, but it's not always the same hard stuff and I haven't always done it the same way. I wanted to write this book not because I have exclusive, special knowledge of how to do this kind of writing, but as a way to share my experiences, and, I hope, open ways for the reader to share theirs.

I started my writing career as a poet. Caught between a love for formal and language poetry, I used the rules of received forms to unleash images and associations that I couldn't have made by freewriting alone. As I mentioned before, one of my favorite songs from one of my favorite bands, Nomeansno, goes, "Tie up hands with your chains. They are bound to set me free." Meter and rhyme make good chains. In a sonnet, a villanelle, a pantoum, a sestina, I become so focused on the form that the other parts of my mind reached far into the synapses to set free surprising images, thoughts, scenes.

One of the writers I most admire and who has led the way for so many nonfiction writers, Brenda Miller, published a piece of nonfiction in the form of a pantoum. In Miller and Suzanne Paola's creative nonfiction textbook, *Tell It Slant,* they codified this kind of form and called it hermit crab. A hermit-crab essay takes a received form—an outline, a scientific paper, a syllabus, for example, and cleverly slides an essay into that form. A pantoum is a series of quatrains, usually rhyming abab, where the second and fourth lines from the previous recur in lines one and three in the next stanza. Brenda adapted the form into an essay. The first two paragraphs of the essay begin in what doesn't seem like a formal mode at all. In fact, the voice is quite straightforward.

I'm twenty years old, barely an adult, my belly flat, though inside that belly a baby is growing. Or not a baby—a something, a cluster of cells, lodged in the fallopian tubes. In a few weeks I'll be in pain, pain like a penknife stabbing me again and again. But for now, I'm just a girl in a broken-down Toyota, moving her few belongings into a room in a big red house on the hill.

Not a baby, I'll remind myself later, just a cluster of cells, lodged where it didn't belong. I must have found this house from a message tacked on a bulletin board on campus, an index card with a man's spidery handwriting looking for boarders. For now, I'm just a girl, broken down, with few belongings to move into this big red house on the hill. I got the room set apart from all the others, with no windows, in the back.[1]

See how the second sentence of the first paragraph in pontoum form, "Or not a baby—a something, a cluster of cells, lodged in the fallopian tubes" becomes "Not a baby, I'll remind myself later, just a cluster of cells lodged where it didn't belong." Miller is gifted at layering in writing about the hard stuff but, by making it formally inventive, she's transforming the hard thing—in this case, an ectopic pregnancy—into readable, accessible art. She infuses the specific, sharp pain with images and scenes from the house she lived in during the time, the roommates she had, the bread she baked for them. The ectopic pregnancy becomes a story about connection and disconnection—keeping the baby would be impossible. You can't move an embryo from the fallopian tubes to the uterus. And, you can't live forever in a house with a lot of hippie guys, one of whom gives Brenda the name Little Raven. The essay ends by bringing all the repeated lines together in a short paragraph as points of connection: "I baked loaves and loaves of bread for the boys in that house, after the baby was gone. I was twenty years old, barely an adult. On my tongue, the name Little Raven, a bird that seemed like a sentinel. The pain, like a penknife, stabbing again and again." She takes the physical pain of an ectopic pregnancy and expands it to include the pain of losing the fetus and the fallopian tube, the hope that bread making can compensate for baby making, and the memory of youth. The form of the pantoum allows the writer to dwell on a topic but, because it must change and be recast in a different light in different stanzas or paragraphs, the pantoum forces new ways to understand the situation.

Miller comes up often throughout this book because she has thought deeply about form and is a leading thinker about the form of creativity nonfiction. She's published two books about creative nonfiction. The first one, *Tell It Slant*, as noted above, is a seminal book in creative writing courses. In *Tell It Slant*, writers new to creative nonfiction learn about the wide variety of creative nonfiction forms, including innovative forms like the hermit-crab essay and the braided essay. In a collection of essays on the essay that Margot Singer and I edited for Bloomsbury, we included Brenda's essay, "Lions and Tigers and Bears, Oh My! Courage in Creative Nonfiction," in which she describes reading an essay she'd written aloud and having the audience applaud her for being "brave" to write such a piece. But she hadn't been brave, in her view. She'd been so absorbed in the form and craft of the piece, the subject had become almost beside the point. She writes, "When creative nonfiction writers choose to write in nonlinear forms such as the short-short essay, the braided essay, or the 'hermit crab,' . . . they magnify the fact that they are now manipulating experience for the sake of art. They immediately signal to the reader that their intent is not necessarily to convey information or fact—or to bravely reveal a dark past—but to create the truth of literature, of metaphor, which is not always so direct" (131).[2]

I believe that making art is the best thing you can do with hard facts—hard to live through, hard to explain the valence to readers. I've always written hard things—the original hard thing being the molestation and the subsequent abortion at age eleven. I've written about it obliquely, lyrically, in braided essay form, and directly, as in the *New York Times* essay. But even there, just like Miller, in writing it, I wanted to get the images right. I focused on the cyst that had been removed from the back of my mom's head, the patchy hair covering my mom's wound, the amalgamated mass in the specimen cup that looked a little like a walnut or a tiny brain, the possibility of my daughter Zoë becoming a neuroscientist, the leap between what happened then and what's happening now. This is a hard story to write because the experience was traumatic, but also because such horrible things happen to people in such greater magnitude than what happened to me, I struggled to make it meaningful. How do we get people to hear our stories?

I was at a festival in downtown Flagstaff called Hullabaloo. People wore hats made of flowers and leaves. A group of kids dressed as Loraxes won the kids' costume contest. There was a lot of music and a lot of dancing. Inside the gates of the concert, singing loudly and dancing strangely all went with the territory. If we had been outside of the realm of hullabaloo, all this behavior would seem strange, maybe even crazy. Think of form as a fence around your wild emotions and thoughts. With a little structure, your loud singing and crazy dancing become invitations for others to come dance and sing with you.

If we shout our stories into the wind, no one is likely to hear them. There are so many stories and so many people shouting, our hard stuff becomes just another sound wave. Shaping them into something memorable and meaningful requires, like Hullaballoo, some artful fencing. Traditional poetic forms like the pantoum and sonnet can be used in other genres to build some of that fencing. The braided essay and the hermit-crab essay can add context, research, information, and a supplemental story to help give that hard story a broader meaning.

Layli Long Soldier's collection of poems, *Whereas,* which won the National Book Award, uses the form of legal treaties to cut to the bone the way treaties had been used to disempower, remove, and destroy Indigenous people. In this hermit-crab essay, she takes the shell of legal document and hollows it out first to replace the language with her on language, and second, to show how hollow the original language had been in the first place. Using anaphora, a poetic form where the first line of the poem or stanza begins with the same word or phrase, whereas's strange legalize makes bedfellows of everyday beatific moments with hardcore US government bullshit.

> WHEREAS a string-bean blue-eyed man leans back into a swig of beer work-weary lips at the dark bottle keeping cool in short sleeves and khakis he enters the discussion;
>
> Whereas his wrist loose at the bottleneck to come across as candid "Well *at least* there was an Apology that's all I can say" he offers to the circle each of them scholarly;
>
> Whereas under starlight the fireflies wink across East Coast grass and me I sit there painful in my silence glued to a bench in the midst of the American casual;
>
> Whereas a subtle electricity in that low purple light I felt their eyes on my face gauging a reaction and someone's discomfort leaks out in a well-stated "Hmmm";
>
> Whereas like a bird darting from an oncoming semi my mind races to the Apology's assertion "While the establishment of permanent European settlements in North America did stir conflict with nearby Indian tribes, peaceful and mutually beneficial interactions also took place";[3]

The poem goes on like this. In fact, it feels like the poem never ends, because, in terms of the relationship between Native peoples and the American government, it doesn't. Treaties continue to be breached. I can't imagine a more difficult topic than trying to explain, and then explode, centuries of injustice. But Long Soldier takes it line by line, the repetition of Whereas pulling her story out like a rope drawing a bucket from an impossibly deep and dark well.

Valeria Luiselli's *Tell Me How It Ends: An Essay in Forty Questions* is another example of a story that seemingly has no conclusion. Luiselli and her sister worked with immigration counselors to help interview children who had been detained by border police. Luiselli tries to establish enough material for a lawyer will take their asylum cases. She details the questions she asks the children:

> "During the interviews, I sometimes note the children's answers in the first person and sometimes in the third.
>
> > I crossed the border by foot.
> > She swam across the river.
> > He comes from San Pedro Sula.
> > She comes from Tegucigalpa.
> > She comes from Guatemala City.
> > He has not ever met his father.
> > Yes I have met my mother.
> > But she doesn't remember the last time she saw her.
> > He doesn't know if she abandoned him.
> > She sent money every month.
> > No, my father didn't send money at all.
> > I worked in the fields, ten or maybe fifteen hours a day.
> > The M-13 shot my sister. She died.
> > Yes, my uncle hit me often.
> > No my grandmother never hit us.
>
> As predictable as the answers start to become after months of conducting the interview, no one is ever prepared for hearing them."
>
> (62–3)[4]

Luiselli takes this hard job and turns it into a hard story. No kid's story is identical but the stress and hardship, the loneliness and violence pervade these stories. By hewing to the form of the interview, Luiselli can corral some of the stories while also making the details of them present and affecting. Luiselli adopts the interview form to transform the words of these kids into indictments of the immigration policy, violence, and racism that infuse the country into which the children are trying to find refuge.

Bringing one's poetry chops to bear on one's prose can serve as another kind of formal restraint. On the back cover of Claudia Rankine's *Citizen*, the words "Poetry/essays" are printed. In lyric prose or in long-line poetry, Rankine couches the countless microaggressions with which white people have hurt her inside broader stories about cultural phenomena. Interspersed among the words are striking images of Serena Williams, art by Black Americans, photos of a lynching. As the reader shifts from Rankine's exegesis about how Serena Williams' quest to be seen as a patriot, a force, a gifted tennis player, is seen as strange, exceptional, and even ugly, against a backdrop of white-ism.

> For years you attribute to Serena Williams a kind of resilience appropriate only for those who exist in celluloid. Neither her father nor her mother nor her sister or Jehovah her God nor NIKE camp could shield her ultimately from people who felt her black body didn't belong on their court, in the world.
>
> (26)[5]

This expository writing is set next to sharp moments where Rankine's narrator is variously tormented, even if in ostensibly "small" ways, nearly everywhere she goes.

> In line at the drugstore, it's finally your turn, and then it's not as he walks in front of you and puts his things on the counter. The cashier says, Sir, she was next. When he turns to you he is truly surprised.
> Oh my God, I didn't see you.
> You must be in a hurry, you offer.
> No, no, no, I really didn't see you.
>
> (77)[6]

Rankine uses the conventions, or, perhaps the unconventional nature, of poetry to break lines for emphasis, white space for the reader to turn their mind around, collage for contrast, and plain-speaking prose to evoke the nearly nonstop microaggressions that make it hard to be a Black person in America.

Sliding between poetic forms and narrative challenges a writer to channel difficult subjects. The significance of the story is sharpened against the strictures of form. My friend and fellow writer, Lynn Kilpatrick, used the form of a crown of sonnets to write an essay. A crown of sonnets is a series of sonnets where each poem follows the traditional sonnet pattern, rhyming in the first eight lines, followed by a volta (a turn) and six more rhymed lines. In the crown, the last line of the first sonnet becomes the first line of the next sonnet and so on through seven poems. In a double crown, the sonnets continue through fourteen poems and then a fifteenth poem combines all the first lines in one crescendo of an ending. Kilpatrick took the form on to bind her prose to the same rules, which gives the piece unique lyricism, structure, and pattern.

The short story/essay, entitled, ON UNDERSTANDING begins,

> *what I know* She walked into my apartment and disrupted the cohesion of our group. We were circled around the playing board, itself a circle, asking each other questions from a box, knowledge which we then squirreled away for future reference. The three of us: me, my roommate, my boyfriend. We looked up and she was standing at the door holding a guitar case. She set it down in the middle of the room. She introduced new words into our conversation: moving, practice, rest. I want to say I invited her to join us. I want to say she felt welcome, but was in a hurry, had to go pack, was leaving tomorrow. Some of this is true; she was leaving. We were a circle, the three of us and she had walked into my apartment, disrupting. Or I had buzzed her up. Yes, I must have, but then, suddenly, she was a surprise, her presence, her absolute presence there in my doorway. *Then she disappeared.*
>
> (49)[7]

The next section begins, "*She disappeared.*" and ends, "I understand this too, because people contemplating suicide give things away, often everything. What I don't understand is the gun." The next section begins, with "*The gun.*" Because Lynn and I are friends, I know she had been wrestling with this subject for years. In the small town in Idaho where she went to high school, a young girl had been murdered. Lynn wrote a series of essays and stories with the murder at the center. But in this story/essay, she adopts the form of the crown of sonnets to give her an additional tool to access and corral this hard-to-tell account. The emphasis on these last words turned to first words reveals the cyclical nature of not only violence, but in the way such traumatic events circle through our minds, seemingly endlessly. Thanks to the form, Kilpatrick finds a center to help the story cohere.

When I first started publishing, I was conflicted about some of my work because I didn't want to be pigeonholed as a particular kind of writer. I didn't want to be known as a writer about the sexual abuse or abortion because it might be seen as trauma porn or too political, or the subjects like climate change and science because they might seem too complicated and clinical. My answer to this problem was to marry subjects together. I made it hard to force me into one category, although now my pigeonhole might be the braided essay or she-who-pulls-together-two-unlikely subjects. But it wasn't only because I resisted being classified, I wanted my story to inform other stories. I wanted other stories to help me understand mine. The braided essay forces me to look beyond the "direct" approach and try to, as Brenda suggests, "create the truth of literature."

I also believe that personal traumas are often minimized. That there's some American sense of "Everyone suffers. What's so special about you?" That's the purpose in writing it. To explain, through as many mechanisms as possible, why this experience matters. It's not that surviving the hard stuff makes us special—it's that writing about the hard stuff can help us, and others, understand what underlying systems made it possible for the hard stuff to happen.

Andrea Munro, the daughter of Alice Munro—Nobel Prize for Literature and Man Booker Award winner—accused her mother of staying with her stepfather even after he was convicted for molesting her. Writers across the world were horrified that this beloved short-story writer could have abandoned her daughter like this. Andrea wrote a detailed essay about what happened and how the molestation and her mother's neglect affected her entire life. At some point, she becomes completely estranged from her entire family—even her siblings. Andrea, because of her mother's regard and fame, had a huge platform. She could bring attention to her hard situation with a short piece. Readers struggled to understand how a writer they so admired for her careful writing and deep understanding of her characters had not cared about or understood her daughter at all. Andrea didn't have to write in a formally extensive way because the grist between what we had believed about Munro and what we now knew rubbed hard. Munro is famous. She had a big reach, and thus, so did the story. But not all of us have the reach that fame provides. We need to extend ourselves through our writing—make as many tunnels, nodes, bridges, roads, paths that we can through any means we can.

If we write our hard things using tools like braided essays that weave our personal stories with science or history or politics, use objects as a lens through which to view our narratives, or conceive how metaphor can convey the depth and meaning of what how our hard stuff has made us, we have stretched our stories to the outer limits. Through formal experiments and well-honed tools of the craft, the myriad ways we work to tell our stories can connect us to each other.

I believe that stories are the key to connection. I believe stories cut chinks in the wall of structural inequities in our country and in the world. I also think stories make more of the world that we know, bringing us closer to the animals, the ecosystems, the microprocesses of our planet. Besides trying to make space for other stories as a teacher, I serve as the series editor for Crux, a literary nonfiction imprint for the University of Georgia Press. I receive about 200 manuscripts a year from which I can choose two to four (sometimes five, if I'm really, really persuasive). I wish I could say this was an easy job—that the four obviously rise to the top. But at least half of the manuscripts are publish-worthy. To choose the manuscripts I will send to the acquisitions editor, I must take into account what the series is meant to be. The tagline for the series reads,

> Named for intersections, and for the heart of the matter, Crux publishes literary nonfiction by diverse writers working in a variety of modes, including personal and lyric essay, memoir, cultural meditation, and literary journalism. Both intelligent and accessible, its books are intended for general readers, including writers, teachers of writing, and students. The series particularly values engagement with the world, dedication to craft, precision, and playfulness with form and language.

John Griswold, the first editor of Crux, wrote for *Essay Daily* a brilliant description of what kind of manuscripts he was looking for. Some of the highlights from his *Essay Daily* criteria for manuscripts he'd like to see, in list form, include:

- The writer's ability to see stories at every turn of the page.
- An understanding that diction, sign, symbol, and image often add up to motif.
- A sense that the writer has read.
- Language as precision, compression, deadly in its effect. Caesura, a term I've hijacked from poetry, for the pause to breathe, savor, ruminate, admire.

- Turning inward for the purpose of, say, memoir, the corollary might be: Not a whiff of self-pity, which is an odorous shitstain on our souls. If Primo Levi can write without self-pity, surely I can too.
- Emerson turned inward: Humility for our provincial selves in the range of human scale.

Truly, you should read the whole post in *Essay Daily* because it's as evocative, funny, and wide-ranging as Crux's books themselves are meant to be. As I took the baton from him and from his co-editor, Valerie Boyd, I kept this list of qualities we'd most like to see close by. But now that I've been editing the series for two and a half years and have looked back at the books I've chosen, as well as the ones awaiting my decision in the queue, I see that I've added my own perspective to which manuscripts I champion. Most of them are not straightforward memoir. So many of the memoirs I receive are beautifully written, narratively enticing, and invested in exploring how their unique story sheds light upon the culture in which their narrators are raised. The nonfiction manuscripts that we publish use distinctive lenses through which the author can shape, and the writer can understand how an individual life makes an impact on the world.

For example, in a Crux book selected before I became series editor, but one I champion as exemplar of what the series should be, is Lawrence Lenhart's *Backvalley Ferrets: A Rewilding of the Colorado Plateau*. Lenhart investigates how ferrets, thought to be extinct, reappeared in parts of the west and inspired reintroduction efforts, habitat restoration, and in vitro reproduction efforts. Lenhart blends this story with the question of whether, in the time of climate change, should he and his wife start a family. Not only do these two stories parallel each other, but they also crash into each other as wild lands are fought over, as female ferrets are inseminated, and when Lenhart nearly misses his first child's birth because he's busy chasing ferrets with a flashlight in the middle of the night.

Place can serve as a great lens for honing your story, offering significance through history, environment, socio-economic context, and change over time. I was lucky to select Brooke Champagne's *Nola Face*, which is about a young Latina woman writing, teaching, and balancing motherhood. But it's also about New Orleans. We learn how the city has shaped the narrator and how the narrator, has, through her humor and tenacity, done a bit to shape it. Cliff Thompson's *Jazz June* reinvents the strange and unpredictable places his life as a Black man in the United States has taken him. Joseph Geha's *Kitchen Arabic* is about immigrating to the US, but it's also so deeply infused with recipes and the joy of eating that the reader can balance the hardship of learning a new culture, a new language while holding a line (in this case via Skype) to your homeland.

Another lens might be uniting a group of essays under a common theme. Lydia Paar's *The Exit Is the Entrance* traces the coming-of-age story as much as any Bildungsroman but does so by featuring each job she's had in scenic, often funny, sometimes scary, detail. Maddie Norris's *The Wet Wound* explores her father's grief through the lens of wound care. The medical facts let the narrator linger in the vocabulary of wound care as we understand how the narrator begins to heal from violent despair.

As a reader of manuscripts, I find the kinds of structures and forms upon which writers hang their difficult stories infinitely fascinating. It's ambitious to want to expand the ways of telling your stories. As I explain the forms I've used—like the braided essays or objects as lenses that increase the available reality that I describe in the next few chapters—I hope at least one of these, or maybe even each of them, offers you a way to turn your hard stuff into story and to connect that story with others.

Notes

1 Layli Long Soldier, *Whereas*, Graywolf Press (2017).
2 Brenda Miller, *Bending Genre*, 2nd ed., Bloomsbury Publishing (2023).
3 Valeria Luiselli, *Tell Me How It Ends: An Essay in 40 Questions*, Coffee House Press (2017).
4 Claudia Rankine, *Citizen*, Graywolf Press (2014).
5 Ibid.
6 Ibid.
7 Lynn Kilpatrick, *In the House*, FC2 Press (2011).
  https://www.essaydaily.org/2015/05/john-griswold-best-kind-of-entertainment.html.

Chapter 5

THE BRAIDED ESSAY

The braided essay allows two stories to create meaning through contrast and comparison. It also allows the writer to see their story from an external perspective. If one is writing about difficult subject matter, by pairing it with more informative research-based writing, one can establish distance on the matter and begin to see new elements arise between the two stories. This leads to surprising insights made possible through careful story pairing.

This chapter shows how toggling back and forth between subjects can simultaneously give the reader a break from writing about the hard subjects and help them to go deeper by finding angles and details in their research that help them think about their personal story, and vice versa. As I noted before, Claudia Rankine's hybrid collection *Citizen* toggles between narratives of difficult-to-hear and probably difficult-to-write microaggressions with cultural insight of people like Serena Williams, giving us a fuller story of racism in the US. Robin Wall Kimmerer's *Braiding Sweetgrass*, from which the essay "The Teaching of Grasses" is taken, serves as a synecdoche for how the book brings together personal narratives about her life and culture with her ecological background and her traditional ways of knowing. The title itself, *Braiding Sweetgrass* exhibits the form of the entire book as she goes back and forth between her personal story of her job and her children and the research she's accomplished, both academically and from the elders she has followed and honored.

The braided essay isn't a new form. In fact, I think nearly every essay uses a kind of braiding—for example, Michael Lewis, a writer not known for his unconventional use of form, wrote for *The Washington Post* about Chris Mark, a Department of Labor employee who won a Sammie. A Sammie is an award given to government workers whose unseen labor makes a difference in the world. Chris Mark invented new tunnel structures for mines. Interwoven with Mark's technological inventions, Lewis describes Mark's father's work at Princeton where he reverse-engineered how architects of the great cathedrals built such seemingly impossible constructions. Terry Tempest Williams' *Refuge* toggles back and forth between the story of the Bear Lake Bird Refuge and her mother's cancer. She weaves together the idea that environments, personal and global, are inextricably related. That the way the cancer moves, conversations move, diagnoses, hope, healing and death move, parallel the movements of the plover, the seagull, the long-billed curlew.

In my own work, to convey complicated intersections of story and research, I tangle and untangle, charge with focus, and entertain with humor in order to write about hard stuff like trauma, the environment, or politics in a non-preaching, non-threatening tone. I use multiple threads to acknowledge that my personal trauma is one lens through which I see the world, and that images, objects, and stories beyond the personal provide additional lenses. A writer's purpose is to connect abstract ideas to real world examples. In my own work, the material images—trees, bodies, animals, and objects—are counterpart to ethereal, abstract ideas like social change, cultural embeddedness, and political forces.

I was born in Salt Lake City, Utah. The nouns in that sentence define nearly all of my writing. I write from a first-person point of view with an "I" but from a place that defines and makes that I—I am more Salt and Lake and City than I am a singular I. Salt is a noun but here it an adjective, describing a kind of lake. It also describes a kind of writing—irreverent—maybe even sailor like. The lake part is a misnomer if the word lake suggests to you potable water and schools of fish. That lake is an undrinkable one. The city part, until recently, didn't seem to capture the feel of the town. Tumbleweeds still roll down state street—street number one on a laid-out grid. Perfect square, each road big enough to turn an oxcart around. The city seems like more of a map of a city than a city itself.

Salt Lake City is an intense kind of place. The Mormon Church dominates most of everything—or at least it did while I was growing up. Or seemed to. My parents, having both been raised in the church, then having left Utah so my dad could go to grad school in New York City, thought that Mormonism stifled their hippy ways. They would have stayed in New York, but the job market was weak and my dad, a geological engineer, found a job with his grandfather's drill-bit diamond company back in Salt Lake. Although reliant on neither Salt nor Lake, drilling oil is always geological.

Geology, or at least the results of geological formations, brings a lot of people to Utah. Brigham Young, the second president of the Church of Latter-Day Saints, after trekking up the Rocky Mountains, wended his way down through what is now called Emigration Canyon, saw the vast bowl that was Salt Lake Valley and declared "This Is the Place." No matter that the big body of water that would have suggested to any pioneer that this valley was a good place to start a new civilization turned out to be full of salt. The mountain streams compensated for his misunderstanding of the lake. The glaciers that cut the canyon through which Brigham Young descended, and the seven other canyons of the Wasatch Mountains, would supply the pioneers with enough water to turn this desert into a Midwestern oasis, but with less persecution than they had suffered in Illinois and Missouri.

The glaciers that cut through those canyons, the rivers that flowed between banks of granite cut by those glaciers, the water that irrigated farms and chchchchchhed out of lawn sprinklers, the river Jordan that collected all the canyon streams and their attendant sewage and pollutants into one and funneled those leftovers into the stagnant Great Salt Lake were powerful forces. The Mormon church, manifest destiny, and nineteenth-century revivalist culture planned to be equally powerful at shaping those mountains and those rivers into doing their behest. Orchards and gardens, fountains and trees.

The church pushed, tucking rivers underground, turning a brown valley green, pumping water up and down and around the valley until it looked like a kind of Eden—a green Zion. Sometimes, though, the mountains pushed back. In 1983, 700 inches of snow fell, rather than the usual 300. That spring, rain compounded the melting snow and those oxcart-wide streets turned to river. As much as the Mormons had sculpted those mountains to fit their grid, the mountains did their bit to undo it.

The geological forces that shaped the city, and the work the church did to shape the geology, played out on the body and the psyche of the Mormon children. Or, at least, this Mormon child. Technically, I was Mormon, if only by relation. My grandmothers were both LDS, my parents both baptized although I never was. I went to church on Sundays only when I slept over at my grandma's on Saturday nights. School was mostly fine, except when it wasn't and my friends couldn't come over to play because my parents drank wine or when my friends went to after-school church activities like Mutual, a program young Mormon men and women attended, and I went over to the non-Mormon neighbor's house where my body got shaped further by the neighborhood boys. The hard stuff came in the form of salt and mountain, the babysitter and the dominant culture.

Forces that shape your childhood parallel forces that shape the natural world. That should be an easy enough metaphor to make. But add toxins to the mix and you have a ready-made drama on your hands. In Salt Lake, drought presses down from the parching August sky. Mercury and nitrates trickle downstream, layering the Great Salt Lake with bird-killing bands of poison. Oil refineries hidden behind the folds of the mountain spew layers of carbon that combine with the parching sky to stave the clouds off. In Salt Lake, there used to be rain in August. Combine that dark narrative with one about a girl who was born in that same valley, whose friends weren't allowed to come to her house because she wasn't a member of the predominant religion. Add a trickle of paternal alcoholism. Layer that with a band of sexual abuse (depravity). Press those layers together in memory's time-lapse. Let sit for a few years. Start writing. Start digging.

In my book *Quench Your Thirst with Salt*, in an essay about a landslide that happened after those 700 inches of snow melted and changed the landscape of many parts of Utah and about the hernia I developed from carrying my twin sisters around, I braid together scenes of land and scenes of body in an essay called "Thistle landside".

> Symptom: I was showering in my mom and dad's bathroom when my mom opened the shower curtain to hand me a washcloth and noticed the lump. She asked how long it had been there. I did not like her looking at my vagina. I told her as much. But she kept looking anyway. I told her I was OK and showed her my neat trick. If you pushed on the lump, it went away. I thought she would like that—it was a little like ironing—press it down and the protruding wrinkle goes away. She did not like it. She called the doctor.

> Symptom: For a while, those floods transformed the riverbeds and the canyon floors, but the most dramatic changes came from underneath. As the water sopped into the sandy ground far above in the mountains, the underlying valley aquifers began to fill. The aquifer just above Thistle filled to the brink and then it bubbled over like any lid that tries too hard to hold the contents of its burgeoning cup. The land that capped the groundwater spectacularly split from the underlying ground and steamed right into the town of Thistle. Thistle— dry, pokey, brittle. Nothing wet about it. Not usually. Not until 1983 when the rules changed, and the lid was no longer tight enough and the cup no longer big enough and the whole side of the mountain shifted its weight up and over and then down on the town of Thistle.

How literally can you take the metaphor between land and the body? My body houses a number of species of mite and yeast and bacterium, and occasionally another human body. A chemical imbalance of any sort can disrupt that number, but even if I manage to kill all the mites off of *my* eyelashes, if they were to go extinct all over me, six billion other human-planets would continue to sustain the very same species of mite. The earth, though it may have six billion other brothers and sisters in the universe, as far as we know, is the only one to house anywhere from one-and-a-half to six million species on it. See how a body repairs itself. See how a planet does.

What is creative nonfiction writing but the shaping and reshaping of self against fact? You take a personal story and give it syntax, grammar, language, punctuation. The simple fact of putting it on paper has reshaped it. But now you've got to give it context, associate meaning to it. So next to that personal story, you set a paragraph about apples, or condoms, or chickens, or gun violence. Suddenly, your personal story is reshaped by these new facts. And the facts of your personal story cut into the hard statistics of your paragraph about imported apples or the failure rate of condoms.

The facts are the glacier to the soft canyon of your own history. You see the history newly. You see the facts a little more softly.

Reality is not my strong suit, which is rough for a nonfiction writer. Happily, the braided essay lets me pop in and out of different realties—not so much manipulating the facts but instead to pace them out, allowing me to digest reality in drops.

The personal story is often presented in the form of classical memoir. Mary Karr's *The Liar's Club,* Jeanette Well's *The Glass Castle,* Tobias Woolf's *This Boy's Life* each strive to build that childhood experience into representative meaning—the narrative develops as a Bildungsroman, a coming-of-age story made salient because of the trauma the narrator sustained. I lived and went on to write a memoir. So can you, they say. There's a self-help quality to the memoir. You must have survived something, and, usually quit some bad habit, to write one. You become a source of inspiration. You are the wind beneath my wings. Cue the birds.

The problem for both memoir and nature writing is that the authors assume meaningfulness by the content—the promise that an addiction overcome is meaningful. That a bird, flying, is inherently meaningful. I do think, depending on how you write it, that birds and addictions *can* make meaning separately, but I think meaning often lies in what F. Scott Fitzgerald called real intelligence: the ability to hold two opposing ideas in your mind at the same time. The tension between two unlike things, working against each other, do, with enough stress and repetition, press meaning out of the other.

Environmental writing, like any political writing, can be preachy, off-putting, overly earnest and super reverential. Because of this tendency toward invoking birds and trees and turtles and imagining that just speaking their names connotes their significance, anyone who doesn't think turtles or birds are inherently significant is turned off. On the other hand, there's a whole contingent of people who say, you're 27 years old? How can you write a memoir? You haven't even lived yet. You're not famous. You are not an addict. Your insights about life and living cannot possibly be significant.

In fact, it is memoir that offers something unique to environmental writing. By situating the self in the story, the writer personalizes what in some nature writing might come off as eulogizing and obvious, but when I toggle between me and the rest of the world, not only do I stop myself from boring myself with what I already know, but I also find surprising commonalties between me and prairie dogs or me and gutters or the way geological formations seem permanent, until they're not, which reminds me that my bad habits or unattractive character traits, like writing about myself, are probably not necessarily permanent either.

I make friends in the same way I make essays—through indirect and hybrid ways. One of my new friends came to me in a braided way. The director of the program for which I serve as Writer-in-Residence, Bruce Hungate at the Center for Ecosystem Science and Society, had been working with Allison Langer and Andrea Askowitz as part of their Writing Class Radio. Bruce is not only a world-renowned ecosystem scientist, but also a master piano player and a gifted writer. He and his wife, Jane Marks, have worked to bring writing into their science world in the hope of making their important climate science work accessible and available. Through Bruce and Jane, I met Andrea and Allison and have been working with them on a campaign to enshrine reproductive rights in Florida. I took one of their classes and wrote a short, braided essay for one of them. The form captivated Andrea. Plus, she had been braided into learning a lot about climate change, having worked with Bruce, Jane, and their graduate students, so she took a shot at braiding a personal narrative with a climate event and shared it with me.

Jump Rope in Case of Hurricane
Andrea Askowitz

I pull out my jump rope and start slow with a double jump, just high enough for the rope to pass under my feet. Swing, jump, jump one. Swing, jump, jump two. Swing, jump, jump three. At 100, I raise my left pinky and start at one again. At 200, I lift my left ring finger. It's easy to lose count.

Before dawn, my daughter's college, Tallahassee Community College (TCC) sent out three text messages. 1. TCC ALERT! Severe Thunderstorm Warning! 2. Tornado Warning! 3. TCC ALERT, TCC ALERT, TCC ALERT!

I called. Tashi was up. She got the alerts, which came through her cell phone, same as mine, with an excruciating sound. She did her best to turn them off so she could go back to sleep. She heard the wind. She thinks she heard trees fall. She said she wasn't afraid, but I am. Today is May 10. Hurricane season starts June 1. We're not even in hurricane season yet, and this is the second time Tallahassee has been under a tornado warning since my daughter got there five months ago.

I'm at 300. My comment: Perhaps a reminder we're back to jumping rope. Maybe "My feet bounce. I count. 300." (What a healthy? response to stress! I asked my kids what this strappy thing on the floor was, they're like, it's a jump rope mom. How would I know. We had these weird plastic contraptions in elementary school the last time I cared about jump ropes.) The first 400 are always the hardest. Stiff muscles. Dread this workout will last forever. I started jumping rope at nine or ten to improve my footwork on the tennis court.[nw comment: A little more info on why so serious about tennis in 3rd grade?] I still play tennis, but at 55, my footwork isn't my first priority. Now, jumping is a meditation. Jump and count. Jump and count. Jumping is also Xanax. [nw comment: Perfect.]

Tashi lives in a townhouse complex with other students. The buildings are adorable and functional, but even an untrained eye can see they were made by the first little pig or maybe the second. When Hurricane Andrew blew through South Florida in 1992, at a category five, my brother and sister-in-law lived in a similar townhouse complex. They hid all night in a windowless bathroom with their dog. After the storm huffed and puffed, the bathroom was the only room standing.

I grew up in Miami and went through the hurricane routine a couple of times. We filled the tub and taped up our windows, but in 24 years, Andrew was the first to hit.

At 400, I quicken my pace. I'm doing double jumps, only faster. Sometimes my knees hurt around now, but not today. At 500, I stop to stretch anyway. I bend my left knee and hold my heel to my butt with my left hand. I count to 20. I do the same on the right. My calves feel tight, but I'm not going to stop to stretch again. [nw comment: Love this insistent denial. (Does it really take this much jump roping to be thin? Gah! I started lifting weights. I hope that counts).] I need to get keep moving. I need to get winded. I try not to think about anything except counting, but my mind has a mind of its own.

Every spring, since Andrew, I've felt the heat of summer approaching and with it a rise in anxiety, sort of like when a dog's ears perk up. Higher alert. Last winter and again this winter, when Miami is at its best, we had fewer and fewer [nw comment: Since so many numbers persist through the essay, maybe be specific with how many.] nights when we could leave the windows open and enjoy the cool air. In January, I made the mistake of watching the TV series Five Days at Memorial about Hurricane Katrina and the flooding of New Orleans. Levies broke. Memorial hospital was stranded. Forty-five bodies were left for dead.

Last week, a friend who'd grown up in Brazil sent out news that his home state Rio Grande do Sul was flooded. The airport looked like a muddy river. One hundred and five people already dead.

My rope is red and black with plastic, inch-long pieces and a cushioned handle. I've tried other ropes—ones made out of leather maybe or taught nylon, like gyms have hanging around—but those hurt when you miss. They don't draw blood, but they feel like they might. [nw comment: Brilliant and hilarious.] My rope is perfectly weighted and missing only hurts my feelings.

Yesterday, I went to Marine West, a boat store on U.S. 1, I've driven past a million times without ever seeing it. I told the woman at the register I wanted an RHIB, which stands for rigid-hulled, inflatable boat. [nw comment: For my big plan for the essay, I'm gonna need another number here. Maybe how much it cost?] I didn't even know what a hull was until I'd gotten into it on Google. I typed in rescue boat. Blow up boat. Best boat in case of flooding.

At 600, I raise my right thumb and step up my pace again, one swing, one jump. I dash off 100 in like a minute maybe two minutes. I'm not timing, though I know 1,000 jumps takes about 20 minutes if I stay focused. Swing, jump, swing jump. I miss. Bummer. Start again. I'm no Rocky, but I go one foot, swing, jump, then the other foot, back and forth, doing my dance. I swing twice on one jump, but count it as one. I'm moving now, sweating, heart beating.

I was afraid to tell the woman at Marine West why I wanted a boat. I didn't want her to think I was a prepper. I didn't want her to think I was crazy. I didn't want her to think I wasn't crazy and that getting a boat in case of flooding was a good idea.

When Andrew blew through, my dad acted like it was a good time to make moonshine and went to sleep in his bed. My mom and I hunkered down in my brother's room, the one room in the house that didn't have a skylight. When the electricity went out, we had Bryan Norcross on the transistor radio. He said, "Do not go outside." I wasn't going anywhere, except the bathroom. Three times. That's what my body did when I got scared.

We heard a crash. The window in the next room, my childhood bedroom, must have shattered. Water seeped in under the wall. Bryan Norcross said, "Stay under your mattress." My mom and I pulled my brother's mattress off the bed, but lay on top of it, paralyzed. I think we both knew that getting under a mattress meant total doom. The air was hot, but more than that, thick. Hurricane winds create pressure. When I stood to go to the bathroom, I felt the air, heavy, like I was moving through water. Everything I knew about the sky, breathing, life on our planet was different. Terrifying.

I'm at 800, now 900. I'm back to a fast-paced double-jump. I'm tired, but I can't stop now. I need this more than ever. At 1,000, I start again at one.

Here are my thoughts, I wrote her. First, I think you should call it *A Numbers Game*. What I love so much about this piece is the explicit understanding that jumping rope is only for stress release—obvs, not going to save the planet. BUT, if you dig into this number idea, I think you could go deep into thinking about scale. The problem with climate change is that it's such a huge problem, we can't wrap our minds around it. What about jumping rope might actually help? Well, it seems here you show that counting the number of hurricanes, the number of warnings, the number of boats—it's the adding up that's the hard part but also one way to recognize how the trouble builds and the number of devastations we're facing. You could also count $$, wind speed, ocean temps. Then, if you want to end on a slightly positive note, you could number the things you know people are doing to mitigate climate change. Heck, you could even just list the people you know and call and talk about climate change with. Something like, "The 528 people I know and talk about climate change isn't the hugest number. But, like (or unlike) my jumping, the number grows every year."

Eek! I love this piece and it really made me laugh, think, and want to respond ASAP. Let me know what you think.

As you can see, the piece didn't need much line-editing. It didn't need much at all except a second reader who saw what was burbling underneath. In braided essays, some of the work is done unconsciously. Word choice and repeated phrasings that the braid forces upon you become the real meaning of the work. Here, Andrea does such an incredible job describing the jump rope, counting the jumps. This incredibly palpable scene is so immediate and intense that the other thread can be rendered matter of factly. Because the jumping rope scene occurs in one place, in one short amount of time, the other thread can fly out into the past with scenes of her mother on top of her brother's mattress, to texts with her daughter in Tallahassee, over to the boat store.

These scenes hold the emotion that all the jumping rope in the world can't quite deflect. Switching back and forth between the intensity of skipping rope and the scenes of the narrator and her daughter's experiences with hurricanes creates so much tension the reader not only understands the anxiety that hurricanes and climate change evoke in the narrator, but it also makes us feel as taut as a rope. I reprint the first draft and the final draft here to show what just a tiny amount of revision can accomplish. Because I had distance on the piece, having not written it, the numbers theme jumped out at me, but the real work of the revising was done by Andrea. It was a thrill to see this very good piece become great.

A Numbers Game

I pull out my jump rope and start slow with a double jump, just high enough for the rope to pass under my feet. Swing, jump, jump one. Swing, jump, jump two. Swing, jump, jump three. At 100, I raise my left pinky and start at one again. At 200, I lift my left ring finger. It's easy to lose count.

Before dawn, my daughter's college, Tallahassee Community College (TCC) sent out three text messages. 1. TCC ALERT! Severe Thunderstorm Warning! 2. Tornado Warning! 3. TCC ALERT, TCC ALERT, TCC ALERT!

I called. Natasha, my daughter, was up. She got the three alerts, which came through her cell phone, same as mine, with an excruciating sound. She did her best to turn them off so she could go back to sleep. She heard the wind. She thinks she heard trees fall. She said she wasn't afraid, but I am. Today is May 10. Hurricane season starts June 1. We're not even in hurricane season yet, and this is the second time Tallahassee has been under a tornado warning since my daughter got there five months ago.

I count 300 and stick out my birdie finger. Fuck you, global warming. The first 400 are always the hardest. Stiff muscles. Dread this workout will last forever. I started jumping rope at age six probably. On the playground in first grade all the kids jumped singing, "Down in the valley where the green grass grows. There sat Andrea sweet as a rose. She sang, she sang, she sang so sweet. Along came (boy's name) and kissed her on the cheek. How many kisses did she receive? One. Two. Three . . ." Now, at 55, jumping rope isn't just a game. Jumping is a meditation. Jump and count. Jump and count. Jumping is also Xanax.

Tashi lives in a townhouse complex with hundreds, thousands of other students. The buildings are adorable and functional, but even an untrained eye can see they were made by the first little pig or maybe the second. When Hurricane Andrew blew through South Florida in 1992, at a category five, my brother and sister-in-law lived in a similar townhouse complex. They hid all night in a windowless bathroom with their dog. After the storm huffed and puffed, the bathroom was the only room standing.

When Andrew blew through, my dad acted like it was a good time to make moonshine and went to sleep in his bed. My mom and I hunkered down in my brother's room, the one room in the house that didn't have a skylight. When the electricity went out, we had Bryan Norcross on the transistor radio. He said, "Do not go outside." I wasn't going anywhere, except the bathroom. Three times. That's what my body did when I got scared.

We heard a crash. The window in the next room, my childhood bedroom, must have shattered. Water seeped in under the wall. Bryan Norcross said, "Stay under your mattress." My mom and I pulled my brother's mattress off the bed, but lay on top of it, paralyzed. I think we both knew that getting under a mattress meant total doom. The air was hot, but more than that, thick. Hurricane winds create pressure. When I lifted an arm or stood to go to the bathroom, I felt the air, heavy, like I was moving through water. Everything I knew about the sky, breathing, life on earth was different.

At 400, I lift my left pointer and quicken my pace. I'm doing double jumps, only faster. Sometimes my knees hurt around now, but not today. At 500, I stop to stretch anyway. I bend my left knee and hold my heel to my butt with my left hand. I count to 20. I do the same on the right. My calves feel tight, but I'm not going to stop to stretch again. I need to get keep moving. I need to get winded. I try not to think about anything except counting, but my mind has a mind of its own.

I grew up in Miami and went through the hurricane routine a couple of times. We filled the tub and taped up our windows, but in my 24 years, Andrew was the first to hit hard. Every spring since, I've felt the heat of summer approaching and with it a rise in anxiety, sort of like when a dog's ears perk up. Higher alert.

My rope is red and black with plastic, inch-long pieces and cushioned handles. I've tried other ropes—ones made out of leather maybe or taught nylon, like gyms have hanging around—but those hurt when you miss. They don't draw blood, but they feel like they might. My rope is perfectly weighted and missing only hurts my feelings.

Last year, 2023, Miami's average temperature was 79.9 degrees Fahrenheit. According to the National Weather Service, that's 2.5 degrees above the 30-year normal and the warmest year on record. In winter, when Miami is at its best, I open the windows and enjoy the cool air. I didn't count, but last winter and again this winter, my kids yelled at me more and more to close the windows and turn on the air conditioning.

In January, I watched the TV series Five Days at Memorial about Hurricane Katrina and the flooding of New Orleans. Levees broke. An American hospital was stranded. Forty-five bodies were left for dead.

5. The Braided Essay

Last week, a friend who'd grown up in Brazil sent out news that his home state Rio Grande do Sul was under water. The airport looked like a muddy river. One hundred and five people already dead.

Yesterday, I went to Marine West, a boat store on US 1, I've driven past a million times without ever seeing it. I told the woman at the register I wanted an RHIB, which stands for rigid-hulled, inflatable boat. I didn't even know what a hull was until I'd gotten into it on Google. I typed in rescue boat. Blow-up boat. Best boat in case of flooding.

At 600, I raise my right thumb and step up my pace again, one swing, one jump. I dash off 100 in like a minute. I know 1,000 jumps takes about 15 minutes if I stay focused. Swing, jump, swing jump. I miss. Bummer. Start again. I'm no Rocky, but I go one foot, swing, jump, then the other foot, back and forth, doing my dance. I criss-cross and double under, swinging twice on one jump, but count them as one. I'm moving now, sweating, heart beating.

I was afraid to tell the woman at Marine West why I wanted a boat. I didn't want her to think I was a prepper. I didn't want her to think I was crazy. I didn't want her to think I wasn't crazy and that getting a boat in case of flooding was a good idea.

Now a warning from the National Oceanic Atmospheric Administration: "The number of named storms is the most it has ever forecast in May ... 17 to 25 named storms, including eight to 13 hurricanes."

Numbers are rising.

I'm at 800, now 900. I'm back to a fast-paced double-jump. I'm tired, but I can't stop now. I need this more than ever. At 1,000, I start again at one.

Andrea sold this essay about two days after submitting it to magazines. She's an incredible reviser. She did something here I haven't seen before: taking two threads, the jump story and the story of the hurricane, by incanting increasing numbers that charted our changing climate, creating a sense of dis-ease I want to create in my own writing. After our discussion and her revision, the title emerged as the haunting, theme-unifying blockbuster that it is. It not only calls attention to the motif, but it also reasserts the fear felt in the body. Each time her feet hit the floor, I know that climate change really is a numbers game and we're running out of time. Again. And again. And again.

The braided essay pulls together stories and subjects, but, as one revises and reworks the premises, the pairing reveals parallel processes. It's the way things match and rhyme and move that makes the braided essay exciting for both the reader and the writer. Who knew going in that the counting the number of times the rope was jumped sung harmoniously with rise in hurricane number and severity? We can't know it until we write it.

Writing about fear, panic, and something so big, like climate change, might seem impossible. But like Andrea does, take it one paragraph at a time. Sometimes, when you're writing, you feel you're beating your head against a wall. That's not only an appropriate metaphor—it's part of the point and part of the fun. This is not to say writing is exclusively a masochistic endeavor. Why do it if it's only painful? But the "wall" in this metaphor is an important element to writing and one that helps to make creative non-fiction a literary endeavor.

I teach and write both poetry, fiction and non-fiction. Recently, I taught a poetic forms class to my graduate students. Sonnets, sestinas, villanelles. I wanted my students to know the forms to help them to understand in their work, which tends toward free verse, why they break lines, why the poem turns when and where it does, and the possibilities of rhyme and repetition. But I also wanted to make them suffer a little. Not because I'm a sadist, but because when there are bounds, chains, rules, laws, something inside the mind breaks free. The language becomes sharper. Images become rich. The meaning intensifies. You only have so many iambs to get your point across. These chains and laws are the wall. Your head, beat against that wall, shakes free newly creative ideas.

Walls are inherent to creative non-fiction. A wall of truth and memory. Truth and memory are as great a law as fourteen lines to a sonnet. If, in your writing, you are tied to the truth, attempting to get at the truth makes your language sharper, enriches images, intensifies meaning. As I said before, quoting St. Augustine, "Tie up my hands with your chains, they are bound to set me free." Or maybe it was the band Nomeansno. Either way, it's one reason I stick with the term "Creative Nonfiction." Even if it's oxymoronic, the "non-fiction" is what helps to make the "creative" happen.

5. The Braided Essay

A couple of years ago, my mom invited me to speak to her book club about my nonfiction collection, *Quench Your Thirst with Salt*, that had just come out. It was hard for her, in a way, to have family secrets spilled all over Amazon.com. But she was proud, too. It is thanks to her that I love literature. Growing up, we had books in every corner of the house. She had been an English major. She scribbled in journals of her own. Her book club fostered in me a sense that reading brought people together. One of the members of the book club, Kathy, asked why I combined stories about my father's alcoholism with stories of how the Mormon settlers transformed Salt Lake Valley from an arid desert into a cradle of green. I answered that the way the Mormons transformed the mountain streams to reconfigure the valley below was similar to what my dad was doing with his drinking—an attempt to change a seemingly unchangeable situation. The rivers flowed down the mountains, funneled into the Great Salt Lake. My dad drank a lot of liquor. The Mormons made reservoirs to stop the rivers before they reached the lake in order to irrigate their farmland. My father went to AA, Betty Ford, and the Minneapolis Rehab Center to try to stop the drinking. These are facts. In the end, the Mormons were more successful than my dad—they transformed the landscape. But, as I spoke to the book club, I explained that the content of my book—that one spends one's whole life wrestling with granite-like forces—paralleled its form, and that truth, natural force that it is, has to be contended with in writing.

When I reach for a memory, for instance, of my dad getting up from watching the TV show *Dallas* to get what I then thought was a drink of water, I envision the scene. I can hear the clinking of the ice cubes. The jug-jug of the water filling the glass. The shifting blues coming from the TV screen. In my memory, the glass is filled with water. Later, when he is sick with cirrhosis, I have to rethink my memory. Was it water? If it was vodka, how does that change things? Does it change the smell in the room? The colors coming from the TV? Yes and no. The TV still shimmers blue, but now that blue is a little darker. The innocent sound of ice now sounds like the dum-dom-dum of mystery revealed. J. R. Ewing's words are even more sinister. That truth, or those truths, combine to make different kinds of senses. One is a new, logical sense. If my dad is sick, then maybe he was drinking. But there's another layer to that sense, an intensified meaning: that my dad, although drinking, sheltered me from what he was doing. That the drinking, at that moment, had no immediate, sinister result. That in my memory, water is water and my dad is my dad. That the truth was possibly different is what makes it interesting, puts some stress between memory and logic, and gives me reason to put the story to language. The language—"blue,"

"Ewing," "ice"—deepens the meaning as does double duty trying to be faithful to both memory and truth.

Shelley wrote in his defense of knowledge, "We want the creative faculty to imagine that which we know." We must turn the abstractions of what we know into fully blown material through our imagination. Knowledge, truth, memory are the laws, the chains, the givens against which writers flail. It is our imaginative faculties that turn those truths and memories into meaning. The knowing is the wall. The imaginative faculties the head. If our heads, like our genres, become bent a little in the banging, it's worth it. We created something new.

As we learn to stay with the trouble, deepen our understanding of what and why our hard stuff is what it is, the imagination begins to bloom. The hard facts shape the story. If I didn't want to face the facts, I wouldn't have embraced the braided essay as a form where one combines research and personal story to press hard upon each other like two fingers against a blackhead until the pus erupts. That is a gross image but I'm trying to embrace the gross. Still, let me try a more beautiful metaphor: like mycorrhizal fungi pressing against the forest floor until, from the strain of both, the fruiting body pops up in the form of a chanterelle mushroom.

Perhaps the braided form is most effective when the political and the personal are trying to explain and understand each other. The process of pulling together two disparate ideas is what allows for surprise. In an essay I wrote about geothermal power in Iceland, I asked the question, although geothermal power is a sustainable, green energy, is it infinite? Will the supplies run out? It is possible, I researched, that an overtaxed well could run dry. The power produced by that particular natural hot spring could come to an end. The parallel story I supply is where I got mad at my husband, stormed off, each of us angry about whether or not the church on the hill was Catholic and why he made me walk there if he didn't want to know and wouldn't let the subject drop. I wandered by the ocean long enough to make myself dreadfully sad. I stayed gone long enough to get really mad. I came home and fell asleep on the bathroom floor. When I awoke, I couldn't find my husband. I went across the street where he was waiting for me, letting it go, forgiving me. The essay led me to this understanding that the relationship might be elastic and strong, possibly infinite in its resources, like the hot springs of Iceland—but perhaps I should be cautious before I tax it.

The subject of the braided essay inhabits the form of the essay. The braided form is one of resistance. The further apart the threads of the braid, the more resistance the essay makes to easy substitutions and easy answers. I write about politics, but I have found that political writing is often shallow and so ideological that I often discover nothing newly engaging in issues that I agree with, and I find nothing persuasive in it that I don't agree with. To me, the braided form is a way to expand the conversation, to press upon the hard lines of ideology, to stretch the choices beyond right or left, one or the other, and instead to see the elasticity of thought. "Resistance" is important to the idea because it describes the way metaphor helps challenge the stultified pathways of our neural networks. Two ideas. One time. It's important because the brain resists new ways of thinking. It's important because resistance is an important political tool. Resistance is the metaphor that will rule all other metaphors.

Is the braided form a broken form? Perhaps. But perhaps it is the form that best represents a broken self and a broken world. But there is something reparative about the braided essay. The way one dips into one section of research, looking for that one right word to express the personal brokenness. As you stitch the essays together, you stitch yourself into the world. The world, stitched by you, is made more whole. I think it's incumbent upon us to make a case for what we believe. I also think it's incumbent upon us to check our beliefs against a prismatic understanding of facts. Humility and curiosity come from the same place. "How does the world work?" and "who am I?" are two sides of the same coin. The personal story asks the reader to hear you say, "isn't this what it's like to be human?" The research-based story says, "see how being human is like being everything else in the world?" Strange and wondrous. Wild and mutable. The job of the creative nonfiction writer is to say "here I am, world, and here is the world, and out of this oxymoronic writing, we are here to make each other."

A Braided Essay Prompt:

When you write the hard stuff, sometimes you need to take a break from it by investigating a completely off-topic subject. By toggling back and forth between personal narrative and research, you can push yourself further and deeper into the story. You can accumulate images and details that serve as a bridge between the personal and the external world. Furthermore, you can see how the natural processes of the world parallel the motions of our lived experience.

The instigating effort is pretty easy to complete. Begin with the story you want to tell. Put your body in the space where the significant event happened. Describe the bodies in the room. Describe the room. Feel free to comment on the situation. Sometimes I neglect to do this, but telling the reader what you thought at the time or are thinking now can help contextualize the situation. Luke, a friend of mine at NAU, said to me about my writing, "You tell just enough. Not too much." But sometimes, I do think I need to tell a little more. You should do so if it seems right.

1. Write for two minutes about this personal story.
2. Then, pick a word from that story that inspires you to learn more about. For example, if I wrote, "When he told me he was leaving me, my heart felt like a potato bug, small, round, and encrusted," I could leap to a new paragraph, investigating potato bugs. I could find out why some people call the potato bugs roly-polies. I could learn if they were related to crabs or other crustaceans. I could find out if they were an invasive species.
3. Write about your research subject for two minutes.
4. Return to your personal story for two minutes. This time, look for words that might resonate with your narrative from the researched story. Perhaps now the heart realizes its shortcomings, that it's able to speak in some dialects and languages, but not others.
5. Return to the research story for two minutes. What do roly-polies eat? Is this curling into a ball a successful move? Again, pull a relevant word or two from the personal story to begin to build bridges between the threads.
6. Rinse. Repeat.
7. Rinse. Repeat.
8. In this draft of a conclusion, you don't want to say, "And so, that is how my heart is like a potato bug." However, you do want to look at those bridge words you've made and try to create sentences from them. Look particularly where the verbs overlap since you're trying to find ways that the action and processes between things converge.
9. Revising is a little bit trickier, since you were mostly relying on chance and your subconscious to make the parallels parallel. As you revise, keep noticing verbs. Think of other nouns that might be more evocative of the other thread. What kind of qualifiers appear in each thread. Can you make something more of these qualifiers? For example, gray heart, gray roly-poly?
10. What happens usually is that in revision, as we saw in Andrea Askowitz's *A Numbers Game*, the deeper connection between the threads emerges. Why is a Numbers Game so relevant—we are counting against our anxieties as we count the degrees on the thermometer. If you can come up with a title that ties everything together, you will be done and you will be golden.

Chapter 6

THE INCLUSIVENESS OF METAPHOR

It's nearly as hard to write about impending environmental catastrophe as it is to talk about personal trauma. Small, concrete images can make big abstractions make sense. To yoke a natural object to a human emotion gives the emotion real flesh. Genuine experiences paired with a political concern turn ideological ether into animal breath. In *How to Plant a Billion Trees*, I paired the experience of what happened to my body with the story of trees in a forest. I had an agenda. I wanted to express how people can revise a life path if, as in the forest, the ecosystem takes care of its population. I also wanted readers to admire forest systems, to take care of the forest that in turn, both by figurative metaphor and literal fact, take care of the planet/human beings. Writing an extended metaphor provides a path and deepens my understanding of both the forest and my bodily experience. By using metaphors, I hope that by riffing through associations, I will break through a reader's resistance to reading about political or personal intensities. As one might develop metaphors while writing the braided essay, metaphors can bridge a focused analogy. But another way to provide access to a writer's individual hard thing is to create multiple access points through associations their readers may share. For example, if I compare navigating Texas's justice system to a game of chess, a reader who is an avid chess player might tune in to hear my comparison. By making as many allusions and metaphors as possible, you provide many entry points to your story. It's inclusive because there should be a metaphor for nearly everyone, although one should also note that metaphors come from specific cultural backgrounds. Not all metaphors convey across all people's lived experience, which is why it's important to be as expansive as you can with the metaphor profile.

The title of this book is a metaphor in itself. "Writing the Hard Stuff" does not mean we're writing with or on diamonds. The Mohs scale of hardness is meant to measure the hardness of minerals, with ten being the hardest: Diamond, 10; Corundum, 9; Topaz, 8; Quartz, 7; Orthoclase, 6; Apatite, 5; Fluorite, 4; Calcite, 3; Gypsum, 2; and Talc, 1. Giving yourself an assignment to turn something tactile into something abstract is one way to use research and science. To turn the Mohs scale and the hardness of writing into metaphor would be not only descriptive, it would be fun. What level of experience is gypsum? Instead of comparing how difficult the experience is, delving into details about gypsum would provide a wide, image-filled canvas where you could paint the hard stuff for a while.

It's hard to write about the potential end of the (human) world. It's at least Quartz level hard. No one wants to listen and we've all heard Chicken Little's overzealous warnings. If I were to walk around downtown Flagstaff with a sign saying "The End Is Near," or one reading "It's Snowing in July: Prepare Your Ark," I would be written off as a quack, regardless of whether my sign is meant to be fair warning about climate change. But, if I try to detail a large problem with a tiny metaphor, comparing Antarctic ice shelf's collapsing to milky ice cubes melting in a glass of hot blue Gatorade, maybe I can at least provoke an evocative image. Although my mind is not big enough to hold an image of an ice sheet that spans 220 square miles, perhaps I can find a representative for something human size or smaller. The mind is better adapted to the detail, especially the detail that reminds me of myself. I'm looking for my reflection in the penguin's face or the nuzzle of the mama polar bear's nose against the baby bear's nose. I need to relate to my reader and it might take as many as twenty steps to get from me in my kitchen, to my cat, to the cougar in the woods behind my house, to the last time I went to the zoo and saw the polar bears sitting on ice cubes, to the image of the polar bear swimming in the Arctic Ocean toward an iceberg-resting place only to have that iceberg melt into milky whiteness, to find the right metaphors to make the right meanings. Providing one example and then linking it to another makes a cumulative case.

So, I make my case through accumulating metaphor. The monarch butterfly's migration is in danger due to logging. I understand that as loss—but how do I communicate the impact it has on humans? The trick is to connect it to human values. To the question "what difference does it make if the monarch butterfly stops its migration from Canada to Mexico?," I say losing the unique migration is like losing the Taj Mahal. Losing the beautiful migration is akin to losing the Mona Lisa. Losing the monarch butterfly is like losing garlic. How will you make spaghetti sauce without garlic? The whole system falls apart. Losing the forest itself accounts for nearly 20 percent of carbon emissions: The forests that act as lungs for the planet have been reduced to an asthmatic's capacity for breath. Losing the lungs means the whole system collapses. Metaphor makes the connection from the environment to the human.

6. The Inclusiveness of Metaphor   77

In his essay, *The Courage of Turtles*, Edward Hoagland, author of several books of creative nonfiction, uses the image of the turtle to paint an ecological picture that shows how we are connected through one characteristic ecosystem. He does not use statistics about the damage of development or the disaster of fossil-fuel emissions. Instead, he makes a relatable human story and uses that story to gather up the turtle and its animal kin into an ecosystem of significance. Hoagland compares the turtle to all kinds of creatures and objects: a giraffe, a horse, a governor on a carburettor. Metaphors are how we convey information that others might not know by conveying something similar so the reader might understand. We also develop texture and voice through metaphor: in creating myriad metaphors, we offer the reader many inroads. Rather than using just one, offer many, as Hoagland does in his story. You may, as he does, invite your reader into your manuscript with your analogy of a giraffe, a carburetor, or a horse. When the reader finds the object or animal they know best, only then do they begin to understand the turtle.

The end of the story Hoagland tells is truly heartbreaking—not knowing what to do with the growing turtle, Hoagland tosses it into the Hudson River only to realize before the turtle lands that it won't be able to swim. He misunderstood the metaphor, so he misunderstands the ecosystem.

> Though we were both accustomed to his resistance and rigidity, seeing him still pitiful, I recognized that I must have done the wrong thing. At least the river was salty, but it was also bottomless; the waves were too rough for him, and the tide was coming in, bumping him against the pilings underneath the pier. Too late, I realized that he wouldn't be able to swim to a peaceful inlet in New Jersey, even if he could figure out which way to swim. But since, short of diving in after him, there was nothing a could do, I walked away.

The emotion evinced by the ending of this piece is heightened thanks to Hoagland's expansive metaphor-making. By invoking other animals and even car parts, Hoagland has effectively thrown the whole world into the drink. If that's not one big metaphor for environmental degradation, I don't know what is. Metaphors allow us to take small things and connect them together to effect a big feeling.

It is hard to spend your writing day wrangling with your emotions about the hard things you've experienced. It is also a hard thing to induce emotion in a reader. Through metaphor, you expand access to both. Metaphor can be the means to reveal your own emotions and to communicate them to others. Van Der Kolk, in his book *The Body Keeps the Score*, encourages his patients to write their story down. "In the practice called free writing, you can use any object as your own personal Rorschach test for entering a stream of associations. Simply write the first thing that comes to your mind as you look at the object and front of you and then keep going without stopping, rereading, or crossing out. A wooden spoon on the counter may trigger memories of making tomato sauce with your grandmother–or being beaten by a child. The teapot that's been passed down for generations may take you meandering to the farthest reaches of your mind to the loved ones you've lost or family holidays where there was a mix of love and conflict" (240).[1]

Compartmentalization is a sometimes-necessary response to trauma. But perhaps if we unpack that box by finding things that are "like" our difficult situation, we can see how they connect to other stories and other people. To begin to write a many-metaphored story, you might stay with the vehicle of your trauma. Instead of averting your eyes, stay with the hard thing. Look at it as Hoagland does his turtle. If the object is a wooden spoon, what are its metaphorical counterparts? An oar? A shovel? A toothbrush. By exploring these associations, the writer not only begins to palpate the multiple incarnations of the central topic but also see how those incarnations may connect to each other and signify a larger idea.

While writing *How to Write a Billion Trees*, I had to dig deep to remember what it was like following the abortion and how it and the molestation continued to shape me. After I published the essay in the *NYT* and visited college classes discussing the difficulty of writing the story and the difficulty of talking about it, I told the students that I know I might sound matter of fact, even unemotional, in telling the story. But, I reminded them, I've lived with it my whole life. The events were no longer shocking to me. The reason I returned to the story was to discover how that trauma shaped me, from questioning the attitude that young girls are appropriate sex objects to why I felt exiled by my community, and how, with help, I might have been able to stitch myself back into some community, maybe even build a better one. By studying forest systems, I saw them as a metaphor of how broken systems, and things broken in them, may be repaired. Because I was so used to being me, inured to a large degree to the events of my childhood, trees and mycorrhizal systems gave me a way to go back in and see what connections I had made, where I could revise or even untie some of those connections, and fully flesh out both my story and the forest's. It even helped me return to the emotion of those events and see where I stood in relationship to them.

In the first few pages of *A Billion Trees,* I write about how hard it is to write about what happened and why I use metaphors to access that difficulty. From the Introduction:

> As I struggle to make the singular moment of where I went wrong into multiple stories, I write about how trees grow in collective, resource-sharing communities. What happened to me when I was a kid was like the forest burning down. I stood in the wasteland of my childhood, wondering where everyone and everything had gone. Thanks to my mom, who found me a good therapist, and who didn't abandon me, I started to see how the replanting might go. The stories of place and how place changes in light of climate change remind me of how my experiences shaped me and how I might be able to push back. An ecosystem is always trying to restore balance. A single tree can't do that. A single story can't do that. You need a lot of ways of looking, ways of telling, to make a forest that resists fire.
>
> (1–2)

And a bit later on:

> Here's a little more of the metaphor. My parents planted another tree in the forest of my rehabilitation by trying to sell our house. They wanted to get me away from the babysitter, his parents, stigma perceived or real. They wanted to uproot, if indeed we could still call the family tree instead of barren stump, the whole family from this toxic landscape and move, well, maybe downtown, closer to my dad's work on Wakara Way.
>
> (14)

Along with the metaphor of trees, forest, and tree communities, I build another extended metaphor out of what happens to detritus in the forest. Words like *trash, spoiled, ruined* applied to how I felt about myself and how I thought others saw me. The cool thing about forests is that they love a bit of ruination. Trash is their food source. Spoiled doesn't apply because nothing goes bad. All that falls to the ground and begins to decay is recycled back into the forest through all kinds of microorganisms and fungi.

Unlike humans, trees do not mark the moment when everything turns to shit. When things turn to shit, they say, "All the better to soak the ground with bacteria that dissolve dead leaves so the soil can uptake their carbon and push it toward the roots of the Ponderosas." They are long-winded, these trees. Perhaps because they live so long. Perhaps because they're full of shit. But in a good way.

(5)

I wonder if I had known when I was eleven about how very little is forever ruined, that every experience, however terrible, will be recycled into something else, whether maybe I would have used that metaphor to feel like shit for a lot less longer, even if I was lucky that the recycling that happened for me was into something green and plant-like. Not all terrible experiences are recycled into something life-sustaining. But, maybe I did know something like the first step to recovery is to shape your own story. I started to write then. I started to turn that garbage into something else—not anything necessarily great, but at least something solid that I could take charge of.

I've loved mushrooms forever and started foraging for them in college. In Oregon, I found chanterelles most often with their fancy caps as stylish as Princess Kate's hats and with their charming, crenellated undersides. The gills wave across the orange ocean of their flesh. Unlike most mushrooms, there isn't a gap between stem or gill or undulating top. But, as fun as it is to describe the great mushroom as a hat, it's the system of mushrooms that inspires me. I love how the underlying mycorrhizae that stretches for miles underneath forests in microscopic filaments called hyphae that send pulses from one end to the other, and which can transfer the proteins from the salmon who have perished after swimming upriver to spawn to the inner trees of a forest many miles away. Dear system of communicating, may I introduce use a writer's dream of being read, many miles away? Hats are cool but communicating over miles is even cooler.

Mushrooms make good metaphors wherever they go. Near the end of Merlin Sheldrake's compendium, *The Entangled Life: How Fungi Make Our Worlds, Change Our Minds, and Shape Our Futures,* we learn about the minds of mushrooms, symbiosis, hallucinogenic, radical mycology, and relationships between plants and fungi. As the book layers image upon fact, Sheldrake proposes the gifts and the curses of using mycorrhizal fungi systems as metaphor. The gift is that using fungi as a metaphor and, vise-versa, imagining human systems to understand mycorrhizae. Science can be as hard to explain as the importance of our own stories.

6. The Inclusiveness of Metaphor

> It is well established in the sciences that metaphors can help generate new ways of thinking. The biochemist Joseph Needham described working analogy as a "net of coordinates" that could be used to arrange an otherwise formless mass of information, much as a sculptor might use a wire frame to provide support for wet clay. The evolutionary biologist Richard Lewontin pointed out that is impossible to "do the work of science" without using metaphors, given that almost "the entire body of modern science is an attempt to explain phenomena that cannot be experienced directly by human beings." Metaphors and analogies, in turn, come laced with human stories and values, meaning that no discussion of scientific ideas—this one included—can be free of bias.
>
> (211)[2]

The curse is that to which he alludes at the end of the quotation—every vehicle used to "explain" the tenor comes from one's unique life experiences. As I used forests and mushrooms as an extended metaphor for degraded environments and rejuvenated ecosystems, I probably developed new blind spots. In choosing this one metaphor, I limited the knowledge base, at least in that case. Fortunately, I had other techniques and other books through which to see my own story. But Sheldrake's point is well taken. We are creatures of our own environments. The Vampire Weekend song lyrics that I can't mention here because music companies are notorious for suing writers and publishers for using even the shortest quotations, uses the image of the trees not knowing they are part of a forest, in the song *This Life*. Or, as David Foster Wallace's 2005 commencement speech to Kenyon College, called "This Is Water," begins with a kind of joke,

> There are these two young fish swimming along, and they happen to meet an older fish swimming the other way, who nods at them and says, "Morning, boys, how's the water?" And the two young fish swim on for a bit, and then eventually one of them looks over at the other and goes, "What the hell is water?"

It's hard to see beyond our social constructions—we grew up with messages and cultural cues and idiomatic expressions and micro and macroaggressions that shaped our thinking processes. Metaphors can help us see our stories in a different light, but we were the ones who chose the metaphor, which confirms what the post-structuralists understood: there's no "out" out there. We are our stories, our interpretation of our stories, and the metaphors help us reach out with our heat-seeking tentacles to ask, "Can you hear what I'm saying if I make for you a recognizable sound?" "Can you see it if I take something you know and drive it over here, to something I'm trying to get at?"

Cliff Thompson's collection of essays, *Jazz June: A Self-Portrait in Essays,* traces his childhood and the places he has visited and lived to explain how he arrived at his current self. Unafraid to explain to his reader how his brain works, he describes how metaphor works for him in nonfiction.

> The moon, of course, continues to orbit Earth, rotating, as it does so, in such a way that we always see more or less the same side of it; it has been estimated that only fifty-nine percent of the moon is visible, and not all of that is visible at once. One great thing about writing nonfiction is that you are free to *explain* your metaphors, and these facts about the moon seem to me applicable to all kinds of things. Recently, my younger daughter—the result, you might say, of the collision/merger of her mother and me—spun so far away from us as to enroll at a small Midwestern college. Since she left, she has taken to emailing us videos of herself talking. In one of them, with her black-framed glasses, head wrap, and light brown skin, she looked strikingly like Zadie Smith. But even more striking, for me, was that I was suddenly looking at a woman. This was not the little person holding my hand and toddling beside me en route to Park Slope's Third Street Playground, the person about whom I knew, or thought I knew, everything; here was a young adult with as great a store of private knowledge as I have, one who shows me certain sides of herself but not others, and if I knew fifty-nine percent of what was going on with her, I would know far too much.
>
>   ("Don't you ever ask them why / If they told you,
>
>   you would cry...") (14)

Daughters and moons. How much can we know (59 percent) Young woman and Zadie Smith? Thompson multiplies the meaning of the moon by pulling it in close, bringing it inside his family. We know less than 59 percent of his daughter, but we know 59 percent of the moon, thus we know the resignation with which one acknowledges the 41 percent of what we can't know.

Every physics class I took seemed to require an invoked image of a pool table: Force = Mass x Acceleration. I'm looking at you, cue ball. It's not quite an abstraction that two hydrogen atoms and an oxygen atom make a water molecule but if you look at the concrete example, a glass of water, nothing in that glass suggests chemical bonds. But, if you picture the O like a big mama and the Hs as her two kids and show them walking down the street hand in hand, you understand the molecule, if not the liquid

Metaphors help convey the miniscule and the massive. When people post photos of sunsets, sunrises, oceans, and mountains on social media, they often add a caption that reads, "the picture doesn't do it justice." Perhaps metaphors have a particular way of doing justice to a subject. As with Hoagland's turtles, the wide-ranging comparisons to other animals and to car collects the things of the world and ties them together. The turtle is never one thing; it is many things. The turtle, as Walt Whitman might say, contains multitudes. This generous connection making does the turtle justice. In writing your hard stuff, how many examples can you find to do your story justice? Bringing copious elements of the world into your story, showing what it's like, how it is, make your story all the more massive, pertinent, and available. You do yourself and your story justice when you show how your story is of the world and that your story exists in concert with the images, objects, and systems of the world.

In John McPhee's *Coming into the Country,* he is openly overwhelmed by the vastness of Alaska. In his craft book, *Draft No.4*, he details how he structured the essays in *Coming into Country* so they fit the shape of their content, which is a kind of metaphor. Form matching content recalls Lynn Kilpatrick's "Crown of Sonnets" that I discussed in the introduction. Such structure also invokes George Herbert's concrete poetry where he wrote about God in the shape of an altar. Content marrying form is sometimes what I consider the ultimate goal of writing. McPhee not only thinks about structure fitting content, as when he describes the order in which he wrote about seeing two different bears on river trip. In an essay about encountering two different bears on a river trip down the Yukon, McPhee doesn't form the story chronologically. He didn't see the bears at either end of the trip—both of them happened sometime during—but because of their significance, he changed the sequence of events so that he could bookend the essay with bears.

Form matching content isn't McPhee's primary use of metaphor, though. He fills *Coming into the Country* with syntactic metaphors in an attempt to convey the size of the place. He uses imagistic metaphors to evoke the indescribable vastness, but he also uses a plethora of listing metaphors, just as Hoagland used many metaphors for his invocation of the turtle. Perhaps the sheer plenitude of metaphors—of structure, of sentence—begins to approach the feel of the incredible size of Alaska. Metaphors that describe Alaska as a "vast tundra" may not be the most mind-blowing, but McPhee builds on that canvas with others like mountains as "great stone skulls," wildlife as "beasts of the sea being brought up by the netful," and wilderness as a "land of superlatives."

These metaphors help McPhee not only describe the size of the place, but also bring a nearly fantastical impression of it. It seems not to be of our world. The tenor is earthly—stones, sea, wilderness—but the vehicle is almost supernatural. To convey vastness, comparing one place to other huge expanses won't get you where you need to go. Reaching beyond the canny to the uncanny pulls normal associations of size from their bounds and stretch them into other dimensions. McPhee doesn't restrict his metaphors to visions of immensity. The force of Alaska's nature is blown just as large when he describes the Brooks Range as "an Arctic rampart," the Alaskan winter as "a long white imprisonment," salmon spawning grounds as "a magical system," the aurora borealis as "the celestial phenomenon," the wilderness as "a cathedral of trees," and the midnight sun as "a perpetual torch." Not all of us are going to get to visit Alaska. Even fewer of us will make it up the Yukon or onto the North Slope, but now we can imagine that breadth and depth seeming as large as the universe itself. What a transporting boat trip McPhee takes us on! And, for the most part, travel by metaphor is carbon free so the caribou may survive another hundred years.

How can I get you, reader, from over there to over here? In 2024, I did a series of interviews about the essay in the *NYT*. The reporters would like me to dig deeper. It's emotionally exhausting, but, with abortion rights being taken away a little more every day, I feel like it's worth putting my comfort and mental stability to one side. So as the interviewer asks how do I feel when I think about that time, I start with words like "horrible," or "confused," or "ostracized," but how does that land? All kinds of people feel all kinds of horrible, confused, and ostracized every day. So I reach for a metaphor. When they asked me if I remember the actual abortion procedure and how I felt, I describe five doctors and nurses all looking over at my naked body under fluorescent lights flaying my skin. "I felt so exposed. And, these nurses and doctors made me feel when they said I was too young to have sex, as if it were my idea, like every forced birther tries to make someone having an abortion feel: like I am trash. I am sullied. I am ruined. The shame that should have been pinned to the boy who molested me was instead pinned all over my body by their sharp doctor eyes." When I explain I didn't know how wrong the situation was, I explain that I was a kid, and kids have wild imaginations. How could I know how wrong the situation when I imagined I was Laura and the babysitter was Luke and this was just another episode of the soap opera *General Hospital*? When I describe how I felt ostracized, I told them about how garbage is the one thing suburbs never suffer. It's taken away, hidden in some rural expanse, and erased from the minds of the community. I was removed, or removed myself, from the clean-rubbed roads of the suburbs to the dirtier, scrubbier underground venues of Raunch Records and The Speedway Hall where Black Flag played.

Feeling like garbage doesn't just mean your stomach feels like its rotting and your heart is a rag wrung out and tossed. It also means that rot and rag and toss have been stricken from the view of the new, and shiny. The innocent and the loved. It's not just the feelings that need to be defined, but the specificity of the feelings, the uniqueness of that emotion right there in that context that the images and objects you choose to relate to.

Metaphors not only get you from here to there, either physically or emotionally, but they also help create voice. Viet Tranh Nguyen's novel *The Sympathizer* is unlike most other Vietnam war histories that catalog the horror in chronological order. Disorder, or at least a multifaceted vision of the war, guides Nguyen's writing. His acerbic tone, such galloping sentences, such swift rhetorical turns, unsteady us. And, just as McPhee uses the form of a place to structure his essays, Nguyen's figurative language policy embodies the premise of the book: It is nearly impossible, he seems to be saying, "to explain Vietnam to Americans and to explain war and politics to anyone but using these metaphors, I'm going to give it a try."

As I mentioned before, Nguyen refers to Campbell's Soup often. Campbell's Soup serves as synecdoche for all of America. It serves as plot and jab. And, it serves as mediocre blandness. Whereas the Vietnamese repurpose the cans for to build munitions, the Americans trade this commissary mainstay for the home-made, multidimensional soup made by the people they had been trained to kill. The narrator, in his arch voice, describes the relationship.

> According to popular legend, Campbell's Soup played a crucial role in our war effort. Our military had supposedly found that the empty cans, which littered the landscape of our villages and hills after American soldiers consumed their contents, could be filled with

> explosives and set off by means of a fuse, transforming Campbell's Soup cans into deadly anti-personnel devices. Never mind that in reality we had never heard of Campbell's Soup until American soldiers brought their rations to the front, where they exchanged cans of processed, homogenous American goodness for our hot and sour soup and rice.
>
> (197)³

Nguyen uses Campbell soup as a metaphor for the trouble with Americans. Americans want something easily digestible, which is one reason for their xenophobia and anti-immigration stances. People from other countries bring different identities and histories to the US.

> The United States was a vast and wealthy country, but it was not the richest country in the world. That honor belonged to the people who had devised Campbell's Soup. That was the beauty of capitalism, the beauty of America: anybody could be rich, and once he became rich, the rich man could buy himself a politician or two to change the rules to make sure he stayed rich.
>
> (79)⁴

Campbell's Soup serves as a metaphor for the idealized but screwed-up capitalist society. Simple soup, so the "pick yourself up by your bootstraps" adage goes, can rise to the height of power and privilege. But soup, like capitalism, isn't for everyone. Later, as our unnamed, double-agent, half-French, half-Vietnamese narrator observes,

> In one apartment, a former Madame Ngoc pulled down from a high shelf a can of Campbell's tomato soup, the label dirty and torn, and blew away the dust, as if she were about to reveal a family treasure or produce a miracle. She held it up for us to see, then gently placed it back, with a sigh, perhaps the same sigh that I would exhale whenever I contemplated the depth of our fall, from Paris of the Far East to the land of Campbell's Soup.
>
> (108)⁵

By comparing Madame Ngoc's sigh on behalf of the preserved, if beleaguered, tomato soup with the fall of our narrator from Vietnam to the US, the narrator turns his sardonic wit not on a dime but on the cheap tin of a soup can. But, even though Vietnam "fell," America is no

6. The Inclusiveness of Metaphor   87

Vietnam. America is tomatoes from a summer past, boiled with a half ton of salt.

It's not only Campbell's Soup that presents available metaphors and leitmotifs. Nguyen pushes that availability to the brink and then casts and recasts them for his needs. Recurrent images and phrases are delightful and strange. But for Nguyen, metaphor not only connects what we think we know with something we don't, but also shows that connection to be a bit screwy, off, and a tad ridiculous. The more one stretches the vehicle and the tenor, or covers the distance between chapters, or winds the meaning one twist further than anyone thought it could go, the repeated objects lend themselves to humor. Campbell's Soup may just sometimes be soup. At other times, it is the trope for which all Americanness can stuff itself into.

Nguyen draws squid into his metaphor net with just as much versatility. Sometimes, the squid is a metaphor for slimy: "The man wept for his wife, his face streaked with tears as shiny as the mucus on a squid's body" (331).[6] Sometimes, it's a metaphor for abundance: "We grabbed handfuls of noodles and stuffed ourselves, preparing to go out into the humidity, the eternal summer, the sweat on our skins as copious as the seawater exuded by the squid we had watched being grilled" (134).[7] And, sometimes a squid is just a squid, turned to food: "I dipped a grilled squid tentacle into a bowl of fish sauce and ate it, savoring the chewiness, the smokiness, the salty sweetness" (109).[8] "We paused at a street vendor selling squid cakes, and I bought a couple for a handful of đồng" (134).[9]

Some of the metaphors give *The Sympathizer* an ethereal, ghostly feeling. These tactile, material examples like "I dipped a grilled tentacle into a bowl of fish sauce," serve as a counterpoint, again embodying the underlying purpose behind Nguyen's book. The metaphor enacts the fact that divides are hard to bridge, but with expanded definition, piers, and piles emerge from the murky water, ready to undergird that bridge.

Andrew Furman's *Of Slash Pines and Manatees: A Highly Selective Guide to My Suburban Wilderness* makes, and then rescinds, metaphors of wildlife to humans. Through figures as various and variously lovely as orange blossom, night herons, stingrays, and dulse seaweed, Furman's *Of Slash Pines and Manatees: A Highly Selective Guide to My Suburban Wilderness* takes us on a deep dive tour through Floridian, and, by extension, American, history and its changing environment.

Again, this empty husk of a Florida Fighting Conch shell I've brought inside and balance now in the palm of my hand. Why does precisely this object exist to comprise a tiny chunk of our world? Its studs and ridges. Its caramel and cream whorls. The studs, or subsutural spines, help to anchor the creature into sandy bottom, holding it fast against incoming and outgoing tides, I imagine, lending at least a modicum of agency to its comings and goings; the caramel and cream whorls offer camouflage to protect the creature from hungry fish, crabs, birds, other mollusks, and me. Other colors and shapes might have performed similar functions. So why this precise object? And, again, why us? Why these fingers and toes and forearms and hearts and lungs and genitalia and kidneys and crania? These gorgeous bodies we inhabit for a few precious earth years. It may be that the animal realm, this "second world," has always offered us a precious glimpse of ourselves.

(196–7)[10]

Furman subtly connections the body of the conch shell with the body of humans through the question *Why?* Why are we different? How are we similar? Why do we exist? Furman answers these hard questions not with one simple answer but with spinning metaphors that don't settle down on any single body. In fact, the answer is in the movement, the swirling and spinning of contrast and comparison that approximates where we fit in and why we exist in relation to these beings, inside—or next to, at least—these ecosystems.

Earlier in the book, I talked about the trouble with metaphor. Metaphor can eclipse one side, or even both sides. To say the King is a Lion loses the nuances and individuality of both king and lion. Nature writers in particular worry about metaphor anthropomorphizing other species. In *Of Slash Pines and Manatees,* Furman explains the concern explicitly when describing a poem that compares night herons to humans.

> Oh, I realize, a metaphor, these herons. It's an apt comparison between herons and humans, and a beautifully wrought poem on its own terms. But something in me resists the metaphor; or, more precisely, something in me resists the anthropocentric impulse that necessitates metaphor to begin with. Don't get me wrong, I've certainly looked toward the animals to glean insight on my sad old self. I typically relish these correspondences, central to the environmental ethic of this book. Yet the mood I'm in, I want these herons to be enough.
>
> (229)[11]

6. The Inclusiveness of Metaphor

This enough-ness makes sense to me. I want to understand the heron on their own terms. But there is a way to make metaphor and leave the heron be. Furman continues, in the way of Hoagland, McPhee, and Nguyen to draw out the multi-dimensionality through verbs that feel a little like metaphor but conform to the exact bodily movement of the heron, letting the heron be a heron.

> They don't seem to do a great many things, but what yellow-crowned night-herons do they do with almost mesmerizing deliberation and care. They snap twigs and branches from live oak trees. They walk gingerly across the russet bark and present the twig or branch to their mate, who accepts it, weaves it into the nest. They stand side-by-side to face the evening sun. They preen one another with languorous swipes of their chunky bills, flash their nuptial plumes. They seem so dippy in love, canoodling as they do, that I'm sometimes compelled to avert my eyes.
>
> (230)

Those verbs could easily apply to humans. Well, most words probably can since humans created human language for our use. But while Furman avoids direct metaphor, for example, herons are dinosaurs, the verbs track the many ways herons move in their ecosystem, with their kin, as their Whitmanesque selves "containing multitudes."

Sometimes, a metaphor is the puzzle piece you were looking for as you try to connect living the hard stuff with how to write about it. Jill Christman's memoir, *If This Were Fiction: A Love Story in Essays*, begins with an essay she first published in *Brevity Magazine*. The book is about the time she was molested as a child, about her fiancé who died when she was twenty-two, and her worry for and her children's future. Although grief permeates the essays, Christman also brings a lot of joy and humor. Big metaphors allow for such tonal shifts. In a class Christman presented for Lafayette Writers' Studio called "Can I Say This? Writing the Hard Stuff" (she and I talked about the title of my book. We agree on nearly everything—including that fact there is room enough in the world for many discourses about writing hard things. I look forward to her version of this book's idea), she modeled for the students in the class one method toward writing about grief. She suggested focusing completely on something you remember from within the cloud of grief—a small detail that stuck in your craw, similar to van der Kolk's example of the wooden spoon. Then, she advises you research it to the nth degree. In her case, as she escaped to Costa Rica following the death of her fiancé to try to recover, she took an outdoor shower after an ocean swim. Above her, she found her first three-toed sloth. The essay moves like that sloth. You can feel Christman's eyes as she looks at the sloth, reaching. "I thought I knew slow, but this guy was *slow*. The sound I heard was his wiry-hared blond elbow, brushed green with living algae, stirring a leaf as he reached for the next branch. Pressing my wet palms onto the rough wooden walls, I watched the sloth move in the shadow of the canopy. Still reaching. And then still reaching" (3).[12] If she can meet the sloth's slow reach with her pleading eyes, maybe she can make a connection.

Christman is well known for this essay. She jokes that she should wear a T-shirt to writing conferences that reads, "Yes, I am the Jill that wrote 'Sloth.'" It's no wonder she's famous for it. She does finally make a connection in one big, sweeping move. At the end of the short essay, she writes, "This slow seemed impossible, not real, like a trick of my sad head. Dripping and naked in the jungle, I thought, *That sloth is as slow as grief*. We were numb to the speed of the world. We were one temperature" (3).[13] The essay erupts in recognition. If this were gymnastics, she would be Simone Biles landing her bar routine. There is something so satisfying in meeting your pain with a recognizable meaning, maybe even joy in finding it. Perhaps that is where the lightheartedness to the essay comes in. The "sad head," and "dripping and naked," the italicized *slow*. Once you've found your compatriot in grief through metaphor, a bit of the heaviness is lifted.

Jill and I share a lot in our personal histories. She was repeatedly molested at a young age. She, too, managed to stop the molestation by the worry of pregnancy, although in her case, she used that worry to threaten her molester that she would tell her mother, whereas I didn't think of that strategy quickly enough. She was younger than I when the molestation started—six or seven. Like me, she also believes that writing saved her life. She first wrote about the trauma through fiction, publishing *Darkroom* as a collection of short stories, but, when she was visiting a class, someone misnamed her collection of stories nonfiction and "instead of releasing the tired lie that was waiting in my mouth like a dog by the door, I thought about her question. Had writing *Darkroom* helped me?

"And I said for the first time: 'Yes. Writing *Darkroom* saved my life.' And when I heard myself say that, I knew it was true, so I kept talking. 'In order to write that story the way I needed to write that story, I needed to look into all the dark corners of my brain. In order to find something true that would matter, I needed to think hard about things I'd avoided thinking about all my life. And now? Now the dark corners are lit up.

Now I'm not carrying around this brain that holds things I'm afraid to look at.' The girl smiled. 'Try it,' I said, and I hope she did" (7).[14]

Christman is not only willing to look at the hard things; she's also willing to think hard about things. As in "Sloth," she focuses intently on a single moment. She wants to find "something true that matters," which is the premise of her book as much as it is the premise of this one. How to light up the dark corners? Stay with the trouble. Sit with the hard stuff. Focus as she did on a specific detail from that wide span of sorrow or trauma or grief. Dig in. Do research. Let the detail bloom into significance.

Christman's capacity for metaphor doesn't end with sloths. She finds other animal metaphors to convey her emotions and the overwhelming memories. In describing Chad, the teenager who molested her, she doesn't settle on one image, as she did with the sloth. Chad is Protean. A shape-shifter. Something that slides in and out of her memories and her dreams. He is unstoppable. A threat that can't be thwarted because you need to know the size of and the place to set the trap you need to catch the beast that haunts you and Chad won't stay one size or in one place.

> I don't know how tall Chad was, but he loomed, a shambling Lurch from *The Addams Family*, shoulders hunched forward, pants hanging in a straight line from his belt down to his dirty sneakers, long legs moving in pendulum swing across the sand. He could cross a lot of ground with what appeared to be very little effort. Is there such a thing as an ambling lope? A stride both low-energy and efficient? Yes, I think so. This is the locomotion of a wolf, or a big cat—a predator.
>
> Watching Chad walk away in memory, I see the animal in him, and from this perspective, and the supposed safety of over thirty years, I can almost find a fragment of empathy. He looks so broken and lonely, barely more than a kid himself.
>
> (5)[15]

What I find so captivating is how this metaphor moves around, trying and failing to settle on one image. I totally understand it, and not only from the "how big of a trap do I need?" point of view. When the *NYT* piece came out, I was interviewed by journalists to whom I explained how I had received no threats of violence or even antagonizing letters. The worst anyone said is that my parents should have pressed charges because the babysitter was a predator. I understood that. But it was the 80s. My parents probably thought I'd been through enough. And, as with Jill's thirty-year distance, I see the babysitter as he was. A kid only five years older than me. This doesn't mean he wasn't at fault. But it *does* mean that in an attempt to find the perfect metaphor, you find new ways of understanding other points of view.

Metaphors, especially shifting ones, convey not only what something is like but also the many things that are similar This expansive, inclusive way of drawing your subject creates a kind of ecosystem throughout your whole book. Just as with Christman's sloth, Hoagland's turtle, or Nguyen's soup can, you're making a universe in your book that is of your design. You create an image set—a group of images that govern the kind of ecosystem you've made. You can return to that image set for new ways of thinking, new ways of reaching out to your reader, new ways of seeing your story in new light. As I did with *How to Plant a Billion Trees*, I let the ecosystem of the forest provide metaphors for how I felt my life burn down, how to dig into the decay, how to build back up, communicate support, and even see that other plants have as important roles as trees. For you, to find set of things that inhabit the world of your story, you have plenty of examples, images, and objects to reach for. You don't have to worry about conflating one story with another, or annihilating the existence of an image in service to your idea because you can let the things of your story shift, reveal the layers of this metaphorical onion of your life and connect those layers to real onions, real farms, real ecosystems, real French soup, and thereby, broaden the scope.

Offering a writing prompt for metaphors is tricky because metaphors usually arise from a particular character or situation. But practicing one's metaphor skills is pretty fun. Adages, idioms, proverbs, and cliches stem from good imagery and good advice, but they've lost their zhuzh. Rephrase these common sayings to make the metaphor new and the meaning shiny again. Here's a short list of adages, idioms, proverbs, and cliches. The Internet has a bunch more. I think you could make whole poems out of each of these.

> Bent out of shape.
> Dead as a doornail.
> Don't count your chickens before they're hatched.
> Don't keep all your eggs in one basket.
> When push comes to shove.
> A bird in the hand is worth two in the bush.
> How many angels can dance on the head of a pin?
> You can lead a horse to water but you can't make him drink.
> Curiosity killed the cat.

6. The Inclusiveness of Metaphor

Rome wasn't built in a day.
Birds of a feather flock together.
A stitch in time saves nine.
Absence makes the heart grow fonder.
You are what you eat.
A bad workman blames his tools.
A penny for your thoughts.
All that glitters is not gold.
Chew someone out.
The early bird catches the worm.
A picture is worth 1,000 words.
Cleanliness is next to godliness.
Don't cry over spilt milk.
Every dog has his day.
You reap what you sow.
There are plenty of fish in the sea.
Think outside the box.
Grab the bull by the horns.
I've got my plate full.
Every cloud has a silver lining.
If wishes were fishes, we'd swim in the sea (I made that one up but I hope it catches on).

The idea in revising them is to find a new metaphor that conveys a similar meaning. You might need more than the six or so words that these cliches use. Their brevity helped them become cliches.

Here's one that I tried to do:

City Horse
   In the middle of that Red River on the saddle of my horse, I wavered. I made a basket of his bridle and my hopeful hands, woven to make plain a ticket, a fortune, a four-word riddle—toward blank grass, over moraine and thicket, my ass caught gallop-sore and thigh-red, this low moon night—or to drive, empty-pocket and oat-heavy, toward the arcade, lights, beads, and cover. Take this horse to market or ride him cold & hungry, like a lover?

   No evident fortune signaled intention from out of the sky, forcing us headlong, his hot, trimmed frogs disinclined to march toward drastic, turbid, waters. My election, his obligate—my own toes dry, his turned static. Stuck in junction, we swatted biting flies and declined the light fantastic. The horse's opposition bought a bit of doubt, but I sidestepped capitulation.

Goading, I told him a story about mustangs, the free horses who don't know heavy cargo, leather beating, hooves, shod, tapping on a planet made of glass and tar, only raining skies, not reined in, no carts to tow or the number of him necessary to power a car. The news stung the horse. Brown eyes turned white, he lay his war chest far from the water, His loins hung up and contrary. I brought him here but now; I see our losses. He's sag thirsty and I don't know what to do, now.

I renege. Leave him wet and free.

This example draws lessons from braided essays, formal poetry, and how to increase the available reality, which I describe in the next chapter. I invented this form for two poems in my first book of poetry, *This Noisy Egg*. The form plays upon the rules of the sonnet—measuring slant rhymes that can be read vertically visually and heard, I hope, somewhat like meter, across the lines.

Such pressure forced a number of things to happen. Metaphors abounded—not necessarily because I saw them coming but because language is steeped in metaphor already: frogs (the inside of a horse's hoof that a farrier may trim for healthy feet and balance), horsepower (really a metaphor? Unlike the gold standard that was long ago disambiguated from the dollar, we really do measure the power of our cars by the number of horses necessary to pull one.) Playing with the word "ass," which means both butt and stubborn donkey. "Reining in," transfers the image of literal reins to the metaphorical effort of restraining oneself. "Hung up," plays on the neuroses both horses and humans develop as we get caught in a sea of decisions. "Stung" doesn't literally mean bee-pricked, but surprised. The basket, war chest, and light fantastic signal different meanings. The basket is a metaphor for gathering. A war chest is a metaphor for a collection of money or tools kept for use in a dangerous or challenging situation. The light fantastic is something you trip when you want to go out and party all night.

Forced to find rhyme, my brain landed on some esoteric phrases—like gallop-sore, hot, trimmed frogs and sag thirst. In an early version of the poem, I had these lines:

Horse and I waited on, his frogs shedding black jelly into antiseptic water. My election, his obligation—my toes tipped in, made the river plastic.

But when I really looked at the wording and syntax, I didn't know what I had meant by black jelly. I didn't know why the water was antiseptic. I meant "plastic" in the sense of malleable, like breaking ice through a river, but I didn't quite have the time in accordance to the form to explain all that. I had to delve deeper into the language that was already there to make those lines make sense. Words like "the arcade, lights, beads, and cover. Take this horse to market" and "toward blank grass, over moraine and thicket," helped me see that the choice was between bright city and uncomfortable nature.

The horse adage is already a metaphor. It applies to children who won't eat broccoli and to psychologists who can't get their patients to stop their destructive habits and to presidents who have so much power, but embrace self-interest rather than peace-making or lifting others up. What was I trying to say more than, "You can take a horse to water, but you can't make him drink"? The meaning lay in the lines already. I just had to look for the metaphors and signifiers already embedded in the words. I was trying to make a city horse turn wild, which one can do only by removing the citified human that led him to the water from the scene. It took me a while to get there but now these lines

> forcing us headlong, his hot, trimmed frogs disinclined to march toward drastic, turbid, waters. My election, his obligate—my own toes dry, his turned static.

deepened how resistant the horse was and how privileged the speaker is in making choices for herself and the horse. The choice between the human world filled of cars, reins, carts, and arcades does nothing to serve the horse. But what does a city horse know about rivers? I hope he finds out.

> (First stanza slant rhymes: Middle, Saddle, Bridle, Riddle, red-l, arcade-l, ride him
> River, waver, woven, over, drive cover, lover,)
> Basket ticket thicket pocket market like
> Word sore toward)
>
> (Second stanza slant thymes: fortune, intention, headlong, election, junction, opposition, capitulation)
> Out, hot, obligate, swat, bought
> Sky, disinclined, obligate, flies, biting,
> Drastic, static fantastic.)

(Third stanza slant thymes: Goading, mustangs, cargo, raining,
stung, sag, renege)
Story, free, beat, reined, eyes, contrary, thirsty, leave)
Know, shod, tow, brown, now, now)
glass necessary causes losses
Tar car water)

Notes

1 Bessel van der Kolk M.D., in his book *The Body Keeps the Score: Brain, Mind, and Body in the Healing of Trauma.*
2 Merlin Sheldrake, *Entangled Life: How Fungi Make Our Worlds, Change Our Minds, & Shape Our Futures*, Random House (2021).
3 Viet Thanh Nguyen, *The Sympathizer*, Grove Press (2015).
4 Ibid.
5 Ibid.
6 Ibid.
7 Ibid.
8 Ibid.
9 Ibid.
10 Andrew Furman, *Of Slash Pines and Manatees*, University of Florida Press (2025).
11 Ibid.
12 Jill Christman, *If This Were Fiction: A Love Story in Essays*, University of Nebraska Press (2022).
13 Ibid.
14 Ibid.
15 Ibid.

Chapter 7

OBJECT LESSONS

One way to create an ecosystem of things available for metaphor is to find one object as a planet around your hard things orbit. The object catalyzes an ecosystem. If the act of finding metaphors can broaden your perspective, looking through one lens can also widen and sharpen your vision. Imagine Jill Christman's entire book being entitled *Sloth!* I believe if she studied sloths for a year, she would be able to connect her personal stories to the surprising and immense world of that mammal. In Christman's case, the sloth is so perfect at the end, that its singular use transcends whatever payoff might exist to writing a whole book about sloths. But for other ideas and other stories, using a single object to examine a bevy of ideas can be a great way to touch the hard stuff from many sides

Bloomsbury's *Object Lessons* series, which has published to date 94 books, invites authors to write a 30,000 word investigation of objects like *Hotel, Fat, Driver's License, Drone, Shoe, High Heel, Whale Song, Rust, Pill, Potato, Tree*. The author may tackle the subject in any way they'd like but unlike the forementioned chapter in this proposal, this object isn't made into metaphor—it remains deeply itself. By focusing intently on a particular object, the writers uncover the object's history, social function, personal affiliation, the way in which it can provide a prismatic way of viewing a subject.

One can focus on a hard subject by holding an object up to one's eye like a lens. What one sees through it helps define and clarify. KT Thompson's *Blanket* studies blankets from historical, fabric, comfort-object, small-pox infector, and basic human necessity points of view. Early on, Thompson recognizes that the idea "blanket" is vast —it's a cover, a protector, a disseminator of disease, a comfort, an art. Thus, blanket the word, blanket the phenomenon, and blanket the object burn under Thompson's laser-like focus. Thompson wraps subjects as diverse as colonialism, *Peanuts*' Linus's blanket, her brother cancer, Analia Saban's "draped marble" artwork, and *Antiques Roadshow* under one cover, literally fabricating connections through common themes of security, comfort, and carriers.

If you want to tackle something as complicated, pervasive, and difficult as race, perhaps an object can help funnel that vast topic into a tight point. Alison Kinney's Object Lesson *Hood* explores the way that hoods changed from cloaks under which lynchings could be executed, to the hoods and hoodies that became a sign for "hoodlum." The material and symbolic vibrancy of this everyday garment becomes political semaphore. What once protected the powerful at the expense of the powerless—with deadly results—becomes an excuse for white people killing black people, hooded parties reversed.

Rolf Halden's *Environment* contemplates both an object and an abstraction. Even more so than *Egg*, the concept *environment* is too big to cover in one 30,000-word object lesson. Instead of trying to cover all that environment could mean, he takes individual, smaller objects to guide us through environments and environmental impact. For example, contact lenses seem such a small thing but in his research, he found that disposing of them down the drain or toilet causes this plastic to build up in our waterways, and dissolve into microplastics that we and the animals consume. By thinking through one smaller object, one glimpses the impacts our tiny choices make.

Objects hold a lot of potential energy. One can tap into that energy when one is trying to write about hard things but can't do so straight on. A student in a workshop I taught alluded to a hard story she'd experienced but couldn't write the details of. I asked her to name something important to her that she found in nature. She said, "Butterflies." I was worried that she would rely on a cliched transformation message, but instead, she used details of the black moth to dig into her story about an abusive husband. Thanks to the butterfly imagery, she was able to tell a story she wouldn't have otherwise been able to recount.

I had a big, abstract idea when I proposed to write about my object lesson. While I was writing *Egg*, eggs started to appear everywhere. It seemed that wherever I went, I heard a new story about eggs. I read one about how scientists have found teeth in fossilized dinosaur eggs. I learned dinosaur eggs are round, not oval. You ask the scientist why is that so? They don't know. But the more I held the idea of dinosaur egg in my head, the more questions I asked and the more I imagined the significance of eggs made hundreds of millions of years ago. The shells are hard, like birds' eggs, not leathery like reptiles'. And yet, the dinosaurs were, like reptiles, born with teeth. Early birds had teeth but then they evolved to survive without them as the teeth evolved toward airy absence, just like a regular egg on its way toward airy meringue. There's an adage that says, while indeed birds are dinosaurs, all dinosaurs are not birds. There is some evidence that dinosaurs, whose eggs take much longer to hatch than bird eggs, some upwards of six months, incubated their eggs. Can you imagine being a big beast sitting still on top of hard, but fragile, eggs for six months? Will your mate relieve you? Will your mate bring you snacks? Whoever imagined dinosaurs in love? Scientists say that maybe this long-egg gestation may have led to the extinction. When the asteroid hit, it took out much of the vegetation that would support a brooding dinosaur. The brooder had to go look for food, abandoning the eggs. The climate colder now with the sun draped by Yucatan dust, never warmed the eggs enough for them to hatch. They settled into the earth, which brooded them best she could, and preserved them for scientists on the lookout for baby dinosaur teeth that grow so slowly that they can tell how old the eggs are by the size and weight of those forever-permanent baby chompers. Dinosaur eggs were just one line of inquiry into the egg. *Egg* uncovered a lot of anecdotes about eggs in China, in Ukraine, in Korea. It delved into details about squid eggs and human infertility. Eventually, these stories piled upon each other to convey something, I hope, meaningful about destruction and creation. These multiple visions of an object accumulate to describe the abstract.

Or, one can flip the premise and use an object as a lens through which to try to understand an abstraction like gun culture and toxic masculinity, as Ander Monson does in his recent book *Predator: A Movie, a Memoir, an Obsession*. Monson holds the film *Predator* as a lens, joyfully recounting how many times he's watched the film (147), and how viewing one film that often provides him with unique insight into how the film covers big ideas about male bonding, heroism, homoeroticism, extreme violence, while still giving us the play by play of the film. Next to this play by play, he sets real life examples of extreme violence, contemplating how masculinity is performed and overperformed. The book begins with terrible story of the Gabby Gifford shooting at a Safeway in Tucson, Arizona, then asks a big question: how did we end up the where mass shootings are a near-daily event? He doesn't blame media violence. Instead, he shows how the nuances of media reveal the toxic ways our culture's insistence on narrow definitions of masculinity constrain our views. By watching *Predator* 147 times, Monson unveils how the actors perform obvious male strictures: tough, built, fully armed with weapons and pyrotechnics, with some subtler ones like homoeroticism, trust, and grief.

Lulu Miller's *Why Fish Don't Exist* begins with two concrete "objects": the biography of Stanford's president, David Starr Jordan, and his fish taxonomy. It is only later in the book that we realize that this is the story not only of history and science, but one of the dangerous categorizations that led to eugenics, Nazism, and pervasive white supremacy. And, as I mentioned earlier, Lawrence Lenhart's *Backvalley Ferrets: A Rewilding of the Colorado Plateau* examines extinction, habitat, and fatherhood through the lens of a ferret. These hyper-focused texts show how our interests and obsessions might lead to cultural and political insight.

As Halden shows, it's hard to write about how environment, but it can be done. Environments are made, and destroyed, over hundreds of years. How do you curtail such a large topic? You find a loveable object to focus on—something that a reader can connect with and be surprised by.

Leila Philip's *Beaverland* begins at a trapper convention. In a book whose subtitle is "How One Weird Rodent Made America," I didn't expect to become immersed in the complicated transactions of dead beavers. But as in every "how we got here" exegesis, Philip shows how trapping has been an American way of life for the past 200 years. To neglect discussing the fur trade would be to elide how that trade helped make, and destroy, much of the United States. But, because we spend so much time getting to know and being charmed by this indefatigable animal, if the book ended with the trappers, we would throw the book, and any trappers we knew, across the room in our anger at the near-eradication of the beaver by the fur traders. Philip tries to understand and empathize with the trappers, which shows how expansive and generous a researcher she is. She doesn't come down blatantly against trapping. Instead, she recognizes the practice in the first couple of chapters and then spends the rest of the book describing how, as a keystone species, beavers are a necessary element to a healthy ecosystem. The reader is left to judge, at the end, how disastrous the fur trade has been for both beavers and the United States' environment.

Using a central figure as the focus for a story can alleviate the need to make judgements. Writing "around" a topic allows various points of view to butt up against each other. Working like a collage, one can compare and contrast different perspectives. The order of the stories you tell guides the reader into understanding the subject much as you understand it, without you having to explicitly explain how you feel. Philip notes her interest in the animal early on, but she displays the depth of her devotion not by saying, "I love beavers!" over and over, but by instead diving into the science, the prehistoric history, the environmental benefits beavers provide, the hardship the beavers suffer at the hands of trappers and the machinery of environmental devastation. The chapters are diverse, ranging from "Ktsi Amisw, the Story of Great Beaver," where Philip explains how central the beaver is in some Native American belief systems, to "Looking for Astor in Astoria," where we learn about the avarice of John J. Astor which led to a decimation of beaver populations, to "Teale's Beavers," where we hear about a conservationist who may have gone a bit too far in "saving" beavers by, in addition to starting a sanctuary, letting beavers live in her house.

If Philip's dream was to write about environmental devastation, animal cruelty (and the kindnesses some people showed them), the industrialists and robber barons of the 1800s, current-day conservation movements, and the shaping and reshaping of ecosystems, doing so without the beaver would have been too large a task to undertake. But through her interest in (and devotion to) the beaver, Philip tackles each of these subjects through meticulous research and utter focus on this one animal. By adhering to her subject so closely, she not only threads the needle on of how the beaver helped build America, but also follows the thread right through subjects too big to otherwise understand.

Camille Dungy's *Soil: The Story of a Black Mother's Garden,* harnesses soil's potential energy to bring forth hard discussions about race, motherhood, conservation, colonialism, and survival. In a chapter that begins with her neighbor Pam who brings her hollyhock seeds and cautions, "They get really big. And they come back year after year. . . . Be careful to plant them only where you want them" (126)[1], Dungy wonders why the hollyhocks won't grow for her. The chapter gives way to thoughts about language and how the word *upheaval* "is a word rooted in soil" (128)[2] to manifest destiny, colonialism, and the near genocide of Native people, as well as the demographic shifts and population surge of towns like her Fort Collins in the west, through an etymological deep-dive into the words *ecology, nature, and environment,* and then to the very white and very male history of environmental writing, about which she writes,

> I am angry at Muir for what he left off his pages. Angry about the dismissive and degrading ideas about women, and Black people, and Latinx and Native folks he included.

> I don't believe John Muir or the foundational environmentalists of the nineteenth and twentieth centuries had much interest in me. I mean that in terms of so many of the people who live inside me. Muir took Louie, the mother of his two children, to Yosemite once, but because her pace differed from his, and her fears and fascinations remained independent of his own, he grew annoyed. He never

brought her along on his expeditions again. I don't have the kind of body, or the kind of money, to give me access to the sort of power John Muir preferred. If I have skin in the game me like Muir constructed, it's the wrong kind of skin.

(147)³

Dungy makes her emotions available to the reader here. She's angry at John Muir for his exclusion and erasure, just as she's angry about the murder of Native Americans. Through this story that begins with hollyhock seeds that just won't bloom, she admits to being frustrated about the disregard for nature as development overtakes the west, the spread of noxious weeds like myrtle spurge, and the isolation Covid forced upon her family. This is not a happy mix of emotions or circumstances. One feels sometimes powerless as places and people are "upheaved." And, as Dungy returns to her focused object, soil, another frustration: why aren't these hollyhock seeds sprouting up like her neighbor Pam warned her? As it turns out, this particular crop in Dungy's garden waited until fall to flower. Dungy ends the chapter,

> Someone asked me yesterday what hope looks like. Yesterday could be any day. The hollyhocks had not bloomed, were blooming, were already spent. Tomorrow began years ago. When, just yesterday, someone asked me what hope looks like, they expected and answer that had something to do with protests, elections, and classroom pedagogy. But I'd just been outside. Even inside, the air from outside flowed through my fabric, close to my skin.
>
> 'My garden,' I answered, recalling the pine siskins rustling in the sunflowers. The bulbs I plant four to six inches deep every fall, whose blooms I believe in, though they won't' manifest for months to come.

(151)⁴

I find vicarious joy in Dungy's hollyhocks. Her sunflowers. Her list of garden creations feels full of promise. But it's also this form—this object focus—that gives me hope. That for everything under the sun in this world, we could lift up and apply as many discourses and disciplines as possible to the discussion gives me hope that if we pay enough attention to the individual things of this world, we can manifest their individual significance. We, writing broadly, unveil the multiplicity of the object like a dealer with a deck of card that looks like a single item, then splays the cards out along the table to reveal all fifty-two.

One of the first essays I published was in *Brevity: A Magazine of Concise Nonfiction*. I wrote it while still experimenting with essays and poetry, trying to find a way through both genres where I might claim my voice. I wanted something different than received forms, although I loved playing with the strictures of sonnets, terza rima, which is a verse form that uses a complex rhyme scheme of interlocking tercets. But I wanted to adapt those forms my own rules. In this piece, called "Fish", I flipped points of view, from fish to first-person memory to direct address imperative form.

1. The fish jumped a ladder built of electricity and concrete. Swimming up the Columbia is a lesson in progress. Even before the dam, the waterfalls would have battered her forefathers. The rocks would have packed a wallop, broken the skin, bruised the flesh. Now the flesh starts bruised, already whaled on by 40-pounds-per-inch spray kept narrow and forceful by the steel holes boring through 200 feet of cement. The water directs her toward the spillway. She directs her body against the current.

All the roe she had to hoe.

Eggs were flying out of her tubes like baseballs out of a firing range. Follicular. Funicular. She looked at the cables of fire streaming above her. Follicles polishing those little apples.

Apple of her eye. Her silver skin turning apple-skin—ripening. Dying.

Water polishing the concrete to a smooth, slippery, no holds, no nook, no rub step.

She flipped her body up the next.

Ten more flights to go.

Share a step with another salmon.

She had swum by him a while ago.

Now he swims in circles.

She has to jump over him as well as the stair.

Head over fin.

2. I am 11 years old and holding on to a fishing pole, trolling for big fish in the deep water off Florida's coast. I must have been beautiful

then. Three grown men stand around me. One with a stubbly beard lifts my feet and places them in the hold. To hold on. To get leverage. To bear down.

The other man, with a pair of sunglasses on his face and another on a pair of chums around his neck, holds my hand, folds it around the handle of the reel.

My father stands to my left, cheering me on.

Don't let it go. It's huge. Hold on tight.

Sunglass man pulls my hand toward my body, then out to sea. Following the turbines of the engine. Circling.

The fish, as it jumps out of the water, arches its back. It looks stubbly-faced man in the eyes.

Sunglass man holds the fish. Stubbly man hits it over the head.

No one eats 48-inch barracuda.

They throw it in the cooler anyway.

3. Cooking filets of fish is not complicated. Salt and pepper the fish. Press the water out of the skin with a knife. Slide it across at a 20 degree angle. In the pan, in some oil, two minutes on the skin side, one minute on the flesh.

It's the sauce that's difficult.

First you need an herb rarely paired with food, like rue or lavender or chamomile.

Sometimes green tea. Or use demi glace.

Then you need an emulsion. One stick of butter per dinner party. OK, maybe two.

Reduce the green tea or lobster body fish stock. Or warm the demi glace.

Strain through a chinois. Strain through cheese cloth. Strain one more time for good measure.

With a steel whip, turn in a cube of butter. Don't let it melt. Emulsify means "to make one."

Make the reduction open up and hook elbows with a molecule of the fat. Water and oil don't mix, my ass. Water and oil are the same thing, if you whisk fast enough and if you add the butter slowly.

Puddle the emulsion in the middle of the plate.

Pile under the fish some truffled risotto, some roasted potatoes, some chard wilted in wine.

For color add citrus or tomatoes or little dices of carrot, strewn around the plate.

Let the fish rest for a minute or so. To re-distribute the juices. To firm the flesh. Do not let the fish get cold.[5]

This essay is about agency. It's about death of nature, of childhood, of a literal fish. And, it's about change and survival. At least, that's what I've learned about the essay in the last nineteen years since it was published. My colleague and fellow writer, Heidi Czerwiec, has opened the folds that I tucked into the blankets of this essay—some of which I see only thanks to her exegesis. She generously references the essay in her brilliant book *Crafting the Lyric Essay: Strike a Chord* and wrote an essay she wrote in *Brevity*'s blog where she described how the three visions of "fish" complement and crash into each other:

> "Fish" represents three different kinds of nonfiction writing – nature documentary, memoir, and food writing – with which students are already familiar. But how do they work (or not work) together as a triptych of styles seemingly linked only by topic? Each section presents only a brief, image-based moment addressing some aspect of fish – only the recipe-like third section offers us much closure, and none gives that satisfying moral or meaning that students long for. Their reaction to "Fish" is complicated further by unexpected lyric elements: "This isn't an essay; it's a poem," they complain. While each section has its distinct voice, images and words echo across the essay:

the straining of the salmon upstream becomes the straining of the young girl and barracuda against each other, and returns as directions for making a sauce: "Strain through a chinois. Strain through cheese cloth. Strain one more time for good measure." Words like "circling," "hold," and "flesh" recur, accruing meaning. And Walker breaks her prose into short paragraphs sometimes only a line long, which visually resembles poetry and affects the pacing of how we read her essay. How can all of these elements co-exist in the same piece of writing?[6]

I love this idea of the three vignettes not working. As I expressed in the first chapter, metaphors that don't work can be as revelatory as those that do. Does the salmon's flesh, beaten by the fish ladder's unforgiving concrete, match the young girl's body on the boat? Does the fish in the pan equal the desperate spawning salmon? As the three sections rub against each other, the failing of metaphor is also one of the points of the piece. There are no transitions, I seem to argue. The world is a place of comparisons and contrasts—do we ever see anything as it really is or is it all a reflection in the boatman's sunglasses? As we saw with metaphor, when objects are at the fore, the sharpen vision and reveal unexpected connections, but they also shift like when you're at the optometrist's office and he flips the glass and asks which is better, "This?" "Or This?" The shifting keeps us on our toes.

Wendy S. Walters, author of the fiction/nonfiction collection *Multiply/Divide: On the American Real and Surreal*, the poetry collections *Troy*, and *Longer I Wait, More You Love Me* and a winner of a Creative Capital grant for *Dead White*: a book-length polemic against the use of white paint in both interior and exterior spaces shifts her lenses across genre to write about place, race, and erasure. In an essay for *The Yale Review*, she recounts what should have been an idyllic experience out in the country, wandering through the fields, visiting bucolic farms, meeting people who live there. But this idyll turns less than ideal. When Walters gets lost, she approaches one of the houses. Instead of offering her directions, a woman from inside of the house screams at Walters to go away. In an imagined retelling of the story, Walters envisions this woman opening the door to hurl a can of Campbell's Soup at her. Why a can of soup?

Walters uses Campbell's Soup as a lens to understand what the hell happened in a supposedly reasonable rural community in a supposedly reasonable country. Just as Nguyen invoked that same item to demonstrate how America can be tasteless, mixed-up, and missing the point, Walters uses it to show how Campbell's Soup is not always the safe bet you think it is. In fact, it may be used as a weapon. Walters takes the soup can on a tour through violence perpetrated against Black people in America. She writes,

> Of course, the soup can is not a gun, though in this imagined moment it succeeds in delivering its own violence. A soup can, in this account, is a metaphor for convenience and consistency, for flavor preserved by heat and lightlessness. A gun is a metaphor for the damage the body cannot accomplish on its own. A can of soup must be heated to 248 degrees Fahrenheit, more or less, in order to be called sterile. The barrel of a 5-inch 50-caliber pistol will reach a temperature of about 275 degrees if fired twenty-seven times in less than four minutes, give or take. They are not commensurate, or interchangeable. Yet as emblems of industry, both items are stored within arm's reach in the American household; their magnitude resides in multiplicity, in how easily they can be taken in hand, into so many hands.[7]

Just as Andrew Furman resisted conflating the night herons with humans, Walters doesn't expect the reader to understand that a can of soup is exactly like a gun. But in terms of its convenience, its ordinariness, its Americanness, it is *like* a gun—as available and "useful" as an American consumer expects. Hot. Metallic. The can of soup signals more than weapon. It stands for a deep sense of not being wanted. This ordinary, American thing stands for ordinary Americans that Walters might encounter who dismiss or even disdain her. They get to hold up their can of soup as a sign of inclusion to a club that means to exclude her. Walters writes,

> I offer the lobbed soup can as a violent illustration of rejection and its related feelings. It makes me recall moments I have been turned away when I wanted to continue wandering: please leave this store, we will not sell to you; please leave this restaurant, we will not serve you; please leave this park, you are not welcome to play here; please get out of this cab, I'm not taking you anywhere.[8]

This difference between the soup can and the gun, the difference between soup as hospitality turned violent dismissal, the difference between thinking this land is *our* land versus *my* land, widens a space for Walters to explore the history of Campbell's Soup, Herman Melville, Andy Warhol, the annexation of Mexico, and the fugitive slave act. In each of these histories, the definition of Campbell's Soup quivers, but in that movement, a sense that William Carlos Williams' lines from Spring and All, "The pure products of America/Go Crazy" shine metallic and hard as a bullet.

In creative writing classes, we are forever encouraging the students to "show don't tell," "use concrete language," "be specific!" These are great suggestions, of course, but understanding why concrete, specific, language is so conducive to communicating is complex. Through the study of an object, we can peer through the lens of multiple disciplines. For example, take "Tree" as your focused object. Then, research how that object is seen through the lenses of botany, history, cultures, religions, philosophies, even physics. By understanding how one physical object can be expressed through multiple genres and points of view, you will see how specific, concrete, and material details underpin the abstract thinking behind various disciplinary and cultural practices. By focusing so intently on an object, the writer is able to spend a lot of time *not* thinking about their hard story but, when the parts are added up, you will see how this object gives you new insight on this hard matter.

Object Lesson Prompt:
My favorite way to teach object lessons at the university is to ask my students to choose an object and then look at it from every discipline, every major that they have heard about in college.

For the Object Lesson Series, *Egg*, I practiced this exercise, and, although the final form stretched beyond these lists, making the lists helped me reach beyond my own culture, prejudices, and proclivities to see the egg in new light.

Egg in religion:

- In Christianity, eggs symbolize fertility, resurrection, and eternal life. In some countries, Christian rituals, eggs are associated with Carnival and Corpus Christi.
- In the Jewish Passover Seder, a roasted egg is placed on the table to represent spring and the new year. Hard-boiled eggs are also a mourning food in the Jewish faith.
- In Hinduism, Brahma and Shiva were born from the cosmic egg. Eggs are also a source of life and bring together male and female principles.
- In ancient Zoroastrianism, eggs were associated with the spring festival of Nowruz.
- Eggs have been associated with pagan symbols for thousands of years, linked with spring, rebirth, sustenance, and growth.

- In the Society Islands, the creator of the world, Ta'aroa, comes forth from an egg, which then breaks in two, forming heaven and earth.
- In the Aboriginal Dreamtime, the egg symbolizes the sun.
- In the Roman Catholic Church in Poland, a blessing of decorative baskets with Easter eggs and other symbolic foods is a beloved tradition on Holy Saturday.
- In Greece, women traditionally dye eggs with onion skins and vinegar on Maundy Thursday.
- In Egypt, it is a tradition to decorate boiled eggs during the Sham el-Nessim holiday.
- In Navajo culture, Great Coyote was formed in the water. He told First Man and First Woman that he had been hatched from an egg, and knew all that was under the water and all that was in the skies.

Eggs in literature:
Humpty Dumpty, Green Eggs and Ham, The Goose that Laid the Golden Egg and adages like "Don't put all your eggs in one basket" and "To make an omelet, you have to break a few eggs." Also, there is a lot of overlap between religion, philosophy, and art when reading for eggs in literature.

Eggs in art[9]:

- The eggs across Hieronymus Bosch's Garden of Earthly Delights, 1490–1510.
- Still Life with Bread and Eggs, 1865, by Paul Cézanne.
- Eggs, 1982, by Andy Warhol.
- Broken Eggs, 1756, by Jean-Baptiste Greuze.
- The Eggs, 1944, by Sir Cedric Morris.
- Snack With Fried Eggs, 1580, by Georg Flegel.
- Self-Portrait with Fried Eggs, 1996, by Sarah Lucas.

Eggs in Math:
THE MATHEMATICS OF EGG SHAPE, Yutaka Nishiyama This paper explains why the shapes of eggs are oval, and why eggs stop on slopes. After touching upon Descartes' and Cassini's oval curves, eggs are classified into four groups: oval, pyriform, circular, and elliptical. Because only oval and pyriform eggs stop on slopes, it is explained that egg shape may be related to Darwin's theory of evolution.

Eggs in Evolution: Which came first, the chicken or the egg? Why, the dinosaur egg came first. Studying eggs helps us understand our ancestry, even if our ancestors lay their eggs outside of their bodies and we humans now keep our on the inside.

Eggs in Physics:
Students try to build a structure that will prevent a raw egg from breaking when dropped from a significant height. They should think about creating a design that would reduce the amount of energy transferred from potential to kinetic energy on the eggshell. Some ways to do this would be to decrease the final speed of the egg using air resistance, increasing the time of the collision using some sort of cushion, transferring the energy into something else.

Eggs in History:
"Eggs have been known to, and enjoyed by, humans for many centuries. Jungle fowl were domesticated in India by 3200 BCE. Records from China and Egypt show that fowl were domesticated and laying eggs for human consumption around 1400 BCE, and there is archaeological evidence for egg consumption dating back to the Neolithic Age. The Romans found egg-laying hens in England, Gaul, and among the Germans. The first domesticated fowl reached North America with the second voyage of Columbus in 1493."[10]

Eggs in Political Science:
The price of eggs in China and the price before the 2024 US presidential election and the price after. (Reader, the price of eggs keeps going up).

From this disciplinary research, you could write individual paragraphs. Then, as you elucidate, imagine, make scenes, and tell personal anecdotes, you might find overlapping threads. Reorganizing these into threads instead of disciplinary silos, you can create your own exegesis on the way eggs move civilization, cultures, families, and dinner.

Notes

1 Camille Dungy, *Soil: A Black Mother's Garden,* Simon and Schuster (2023).
2 Ibid.
3 Ibid.
4 Ibid.
5 Nicole Walker, "Fish," *Quench Your Thirst with Salt,* Zone 3 Press (2013).
6 Heidi Czerwiec, "Teaching Nicole Walker's 'Fish,'" https://brevity.wordpress.com/2017/10/02/teaching-brevity-nicole-walkers-fish/ (2017).

7 Wendy S. Walters, "Soup Can; or On Hospitality," *Yale Review*, https://yalereview.org/article/soup-can-or-hospitality (2020).
8 Ibid.
9 https://www.theguardian.com/artanddesign/gallery/2022/nov/12/cracked-over-easy-or-richly-symbolic-the-humble-egg-in-art-in-pictures.
10 Solomon H. Katz (ed.), William Woys Weaver (associate ed.), *Encyclopedia of Food and Culture*, Vol. 1, 558, Scribner (2003).

Chapter 8

Dissociation Versus Distance

Time provides its own technique—with a sufficient distance, one can view difficult subjects with greater perspective. Even if one is tackling climate change or racial bigotry, taking a minute to adjust perspective can allow a writer to make cooler-headed arguments. But sometimes, the writing work feels immediately necessary. And sometimes, objectivity isn't what one wants. Maybe this is the moment to express emotion. To write about recent hard things, one can perform a forced kind of distance through things like objects, metaphors, and braids. But in this chapter, I show how the "author" can split from her "narrator." She can organize the body on a page and, in so doing, gets to move that body for her own purposes. As author, she is empowered to choose the language, the images, the senses, the way she describes the narrator's gait. For hard stuff that involves not being in charge of one's body in real life, regaining control through writing can be transformative and from here, you can draw the reader into the emotions.

After my abortion story came out in the *NYT*, I travelled to back east to give talks from my recent book, *Processed Meats: Essays on Food, Flesh, and Navigating Disaster*, but nearly everyone wanted to talk about abortion bans. That was fine with me. I have said the word "abortion" more times in the past three months than in my whole life. With every utterance, the words loses some of its shaming power.

More than once, the audience asked questions about what it was like to write so openly. In response, I quoted Brenda Miller in the essay I mentioned earlier, "Lions and Tigers and Bears Oh My! Courage and Creative Nonfiction," from *Bending Genre*. Miller writes that while reading an essay she had never read aloud to an audience before, she inadvertently revealed some highly personal material. She had been too enmeshed in the creation of the piece to feel awkward about the content. She had been focused on getting the words right. As she writes in "Lions,"

> I thanked everyone warmly, and I really did appreciate the praise, but I went back to my seat feeling suddenly self-conscious, deflated,

a fraud. Brave? I'm afraid of my own shadow. And to anoint me as brave made me feel as if I had really done something wrong, something no one in their right mind would do: risk making an ass of myself in public. Bravery implied that I had screwed up my courage to both write and read that essay, but I had simply been in my chair writing. I had been following form and language and voice to get the essay where it wanted to go; at some point momentum had taken over. I didn't even know what I was writing until I'd written it, and I'd been chuckling the whole time, enjoying myself immensely. I'd read the piece to that audience only because I liked the form so much, loved reading that voice aloud. Brave? Uh oh, I thought, what have I done?

(131)[1]

After quoting Miller, I explained to the audience that what I worried about in writing the abortion piece was my metaphors. Was the metaphor of feeling like the gates of a jail swung closed after Dobbs too extreme? Was the connection to the removal of a cyst from the back of my mom's head making too much of a parallel between an embryo and a ganglion? Should I begin with dialogue or with the presentation of my daughter as a young woman on the cusp of college, wondering how she wants to contribute to the fabric of this world? When you're deep in the sentences, you don't worry about how personal you get—you just hope to convey and to evoke.

In some ways, I worried that the metaphor in the "Fish" essay from *Brevity* made me into a metaphor for the slab of dead fish. And here I was, doctoring it up, making it palatable. Am I aestheticizing? Am I digging so hard into the sentences that I'm not even sure what I am revealing? What is "Fish" about but lack of agency? What is Dobbs about except taking away agency from more than half of the country's people? What is a person anyway? A fish? An egg? A host for microorganisms? A question mark? That's the hook of the crochet needle—the one that pulls you into the fabric of the larger questions. The tension between these questions and the resultant writing creates complex texture and provides opportunities for readers to enter the text—either to answer or to agree. I want to get at these big issues. I want to pull the reader in. Am I too close to the material or too far away?

I mainly write about the environment by looking through lenses of particular objects: microorganisms, eggs, trees, brine shrimp. In the *NYT* piece, the lens had been my abortion at eleven. Could I do something more important with my story than deliver a cautionary

8. Dissociation versus Distance

tale? Could I make it mean something more than one girl's sad story? I couldn't connect that short essay to my environmental writing. The political mot juste was obvious, but to Brenda Miller's point, could I, through language and details, make a piece that was more than tragic or pitiful or political? Could I knit it into a bigger fabric? Using the knitting needle of craft and metaphor, could I hook the yarn of my story to the larger picture? As I wrote *How to Plant a Billion Trees,* like Miller, I didn't worry about the trauma. I worried about getting the sentences right. I worried about how to keep the metaphor shimmering and moving. I didn't want to lock anything down. I wanted to effect something as sharp as lightning—a clattering of insight that made me, and at least some readers, see something huge. But I also wanted to get the emotion of the situation right. That too takes a kind of dissociation—to let the narrator on the page have the experience while the author shapes it. It's weird that the narrator and the author are the same person, but to make the scene visceral, meaningful, and moving, sometimes, you have to exercise detachment.

In Laura Gray-Rosendale's *College Girl,* the author divides herself from her narrator in the first half of the book, where she recounts a rape. The second half situates the rape in terms of rhetoric. She explores what strategies she used to both convey the actual violence and the difficulty of writing the subject. During that first half, when she describes the rape and the ensuing effects of the trauma, she dissociates from her narrator. The narrator is both in her dorm room and outside of it. She writes about the narrator in the third person, "The college girl gags." How will she survive this rape? The same way she will survive this writing. At the end of the scene, even the narrator dissociates, as she orates the scene from far above, safe in a streetlight. We now have three agents: author, narrator, and the body of the woman being raped, although to use the word "agency" in reference to that body is inaccurate.

> The college girl's breathing's harder now. She tries to jostle her sock from her mouth. Tears are caterpillaring down the college girl's cheeks. She sucks at the air from her mouth corners. She extends her neck toward the streetlight. Delicate spidery rainbows shimmer before her, jump rope along her lashes. And she's sure. There's never been anything more magnificent, more full of glorious-dazzling, fairy light magic—never been a more heavenly beautiful. Am I dead? The college girl wonders.
>
> (25)[2]

The writer and the narrator are in the streetlight looking down at the body of the woman being raped. They both had to get away from her to see it, to experience it. They had to move away from emotions, like Miller, to work on the sentences, to get to the word "caterpillaring." They had to step back to remember it. And to write about it. She ends the chapter writing in mere fragments: "i. am. over." Three periods between three words. No capital letters. The narrator, body, and writer are simultaneously shattered, made small, the capital I turned to agentless lowercase. Are they unified here? I think so. The narrator, author, and body collapse on the floor, as dispensed with and as uninhabited as a pile of dirty clothes.

In part two of her book, Laura, having spent years editing the hard story, having become a professor of rhetoric, having written scholarly articles on the rhetoric of trauma, says of the experience writing the book that she had to write the rape scene twenty times before getting it right. She first wrote it with complete, mechanized, omnipresent distance, but that seemed too alienating. It would have aestheticized the scene, thereby anesthetizing the reader, but she wasn't in the piece at all. She also wrote it entirely in fragmented sentences, without capital letters, but that seemed too affected. It was a combination of scene-setting, reader-orienting distance, and lyrical, affected, literal, even psychotropic, dissociation that made it possible for the writing to be experiential, effective, and emotional.

I've written a couple of essays, two from my book *Processed Meats* and the other from my book *Sustainability: A Love Story* about dissociation in an attempt to demonstrate what I mean when I'm talking about dissociation and distance in writing. One is about owls and sex and my daughter and how weird it is that you can roll around naked on the bed with your kid and not even have a sexual thought but if you think about it—let the idea that it's weird that you're thinking about how weird it is—then you immediately have to get up from the bed and put clothes on. The minute you see yourself seeing yourself, you can begin to extrapolate some meaning.

> I lie on the bed with Zoë who is asleep and smell her hair and think, it's because I'm her mom that I can do this. I can stroke her arm. I can kiss her neck. There is a reason I can do this, I justify. I'm her mom. But that thought makes me dissociate. I hover above and see myself kissing her and it looks weird: too intimate. I scoot over, move away. Was this moving away the beginning of the gap? Is it my own nervousness this where there would be space enough for someone else to move in and make her body familiar? Her familiar body was

mine, cultivated by me. But someone else will find it wild and want to make it theirs. I would have done anything if she would stay three years old and under the crook of my arm forever, but my arm would cramp and her head would itch and we'd both start talking about our favorite foods and get hungry and have to get up. Our bodies usually win these arguments.

(149)[3]

In that hovering above the scene, I absorb cultural norms. I look at the situation through different lenses. This leads me to ask, how much of my own traumatic experiences bend the way I see normal interactions between a mother and her daughter. I see the loss my own mother must have felt as the babysitter wedged his way between us. I see the future where I fear someone will wedge themselves between me and my own daughter. I can only look as if from above for so long. Then, I hustle back into my body, feel the arm cramp, imagine her head itching, and get on with the business of the day, saving hard questions for a different time.

In another essay, "Dissociation," about how we can eat meat even after we've looked the cow in the eye, I write how we dissociate one experience from another so we can live with ourselves and eat our meat. Hypocritically, dissociatively, we can do it all.

Hamburger is muscle turned to vegetable. You don't want to think muscle. You want to chew very little. You want to swallow before you can think about the sad doe eyes. In the face of the accusing animal, you can solidly deny you knew what you were doing. But what's worse? Finding joy in licking the rib clean? Of polishing the bone? Or letting the process happen behind closed doors for you by a grinder, a man in a once-white apron, by knives and forks not your own. You brought only your mouth to the table but it masticates to the same beat as mine.

(109)[4]

The litany of questions points both outward and inward. The "you" point of view seeks to distance the narrator from the reader, but also also accuses the narrator. She's the one eating the meat.

And in another example, I write about suicide and dissociation—how too much dissociation can lead you to see yourself as completely separate from the world and from yourself. Artists, especially one's writing their self-portraits, have to remind themselves to stitch themselves back into the whole scene once in a while.

> In 1948, Sir Fred Hoyle said, "Once a photograph of the Earth, taken from the outside, is available, a new idea as powerful as any in history will be let loose." The first astronaut to get above the earth, to look back upon it to say, "There we are. That is we. We are they." The whole of humanity in his lens. He tried to hold all the humanity, to hold it perfect and steadily with his Nikon. But the earth is more fragile than that. The pictures of the earth taken in 1969 will not be the same as the pictures taken in 2014. You can see the Kennecott Copper Mine's swath cut into space. You can see brown where the once green Amazon rain forest used to be. Where once were sheets of ice, now blues of sea.
>
> That ability to dissociate—to look from above. You think it would make us save ourselves but like the art of the suicides, maybe the picture postcard was just that. A postcard. A memory trapped by a stamp.
>
> (107)[5]

In these scenes I see my "self" as if on camera. The first scene, imagining what it would *look like* if someone with gross thoughts saw me and my daughter lying around. I dissociate and see myself as that seer and jump up and distance myself. In the scene, I am performing the same kind of dissociation I'm suggesting writers employ. To look at themselves. To make their bodies appear on the page. And then respond to those bodies on the page. In the second scene, I use the second person point of view. This "you" serves as both the "me" I'm talking to and the general reader. This kind of you always creates a distance—the author talking to themselves, the reader wondering, "am I really implicated here?" The last scene echoes the difficulty in seeing oneself as part of the bigger picture. Perhaps the greater difficulty is that writers are not astronauts. but we need to pretend to be. We need to catapult ourselves into outer space, look back, jot down what we see, and then try to come back to planet earth as if we went nowhere at all.

Jesmyn Ward's *The Men We Reaped* catapults herself away from her subject, building a sturdy tower from where she can see the hard stuff. In order to make it through the hard stuff, she writes a backward chronology of five men she knew growing up who had died. She can't begin at the beginning because the worst death, her brother's, is too hard to render at first. She begins with a friend of the family's death. As Ward ruminates about herself and her friends growing up in Mississippi, she remembers mothers trying to make the best of things as the fathers of their children come in and out of the kids' lives. She remembers cars and parks and drinks. Then she remembers this age where some of the boys she knew become something else. By the time she knows these boys had changed into men who will find himself in brutal situations, she has moved away from Mississippi. As she returns to stay with her family, the marked difference between what she thought her childhood friends were like and her childhood friends were actually like becomes clearer and clearer until she's finally able to tell the story of the first death, that of her brother who died for reasons she both completely understands and totally doesn't.

Dissociation happens at interludes, in moments of too intense, close-up emotional work. Distance comes from tone—that matter-of-fact rhythm and stark rendering that lets the reader enter the scene by making room for their own emotional take on the situation, which usually works better than telling the reader how sad/bad/hard the thing was. Distance can become a kind of dissociation when the narrator turns that matter-of-fact voice into something a little wild and vivid, like Laura Gray-Rosendale's "caterpillaring" tears and 'more full of glorious-dazzling, fairy light magic,' as she looks through the light of the streetlight and sees something beautiful. What she sees is the mind preserving itself from what happens to the body.

In Brenda Miller's two-paragraph short essay "Swerve," the narrator is distant in the first, telling us a story about an emotionally abusive relationship in normal-length sentences from a detached point of view. "I'm sorry about that time I ran over a piece of wood in the road.... Your dark face dimmed even darker, and you didn't yell at first, only turned to look out the window, and I made the second mistake: *What's wrong?* That's when you exploded."[6] In the second paragraph, the sentences get crazy long and intense; the narrator is no longer just distant but has changed from distant to dissociated.

> "*I'm sorry,*" I said, and I said it again, and we continued on our way through the desert, in the dark of night, with the contraband you had put in our trunk, with the brake light you hadn't fixed blinking on and off, me driving because you were too drunk, or too tired, or too depressed, and we traveled for miles into our future, where eventually I would apologize for the eggs being overcooked, and for the price of light bulbs....[7]

The author pools all the instances of the narrator's adamant and unnecessary apologies. By yoking them together from a distance far removed from the events, it becomes so obvious that she, as she writes at the end of the essay, "should have swerved, should have gotten out of the way." From that dissociated distance, removed from herself, she pushes the whole experience of the end of the relationship into one short paragraph and one long sentence. In accumulation, she can now explain how she got there and how she might see a way out. If she had been merely distant, Miller would have kept the narrator's POV consistent across the essay. The sentences would have continued in hypotactic form. But because she dissociated, the paratactic sentences could lead her. She could make the narrator could finally get out of the way of this abusive man *and* get out of the way of her own self-recrimination.

Miller's long sentences in that second paragraph evoke intensity. Seeing one's experience with that kind of intensity, as if from above, leads to a kind of epiphany. It is a sublime moment when we are catapulted into a vision where it all comes together. I'll never know if Miller created that intensity in order to spur herself into action or if she wrote it to express how epiphany works, but in either case, those long sentences show how she gathers steam to make, or ask the reader to see, that big leap.

Erik LeMay describes the sublime, as well as other examples of beauty as aestheticization, as open-hearted attention, as a deepening of understanding, and ascertained by extreme closeness and extreme distance. In his book *In Praise of Nothing: Essays, Memoir, and Experiments,* he writes about going back to Ohio as a now-married man who had moved to New York City. Upon his return, he explains that he felt like two people at once, or, rather, felt as if his old self was never interrupted. That his old life and his current life were parallels, nearly one-and-the-same, but yet different because he observes both selves as if from outer space. He witnesses his past life and his current life from a dissociated distance. "Every time we went [to the lake] I wondered if I'd entered that pattern, if I was my younger self or the self in my swimsuit," he writes. But that sense of dislocation and dissociation, falls away when a thunderstorm hits, the natural phenomenon bringing the past and present together at once. Human lives aren't the only way to measure experience. Instead of being LeMay then and LeMay now, we are one LeMay waiting for a storm.

> One afternoon while we were there at that lake a thunderstorm came up. It was like a message from a far-off country that I'd once lived in and left for good. The momentous feeling that arrives with an electrical disturbance over a lake in America hasn't changed in any important respect. This was the sublime, still the sublime. The whole

thing was overwhelming, the overcast clouds that rolled in and the general worry on the beach about whether it'd rain. Then before long (there was no question now) a dark greening of the sky, and a lull in everything that has made life tick; and then the way the leaves suddenly turned up and showed their silver sides with the coming of a breeze across the water, and the premonitory rumble.

(67)[8]

These divided senses of self give way to larger events, which is how LeMay at least, escapes the competing narratives. But the act of seeing himself in both places opens up the opportunity to experience those epiphanic phenomena. As I write scenes in my work, I too vacillate between selves in two places at once. Am I my younger self? Or am I my present self, standing aside the lake? I can see myself as if from afar—both that young person and my current, swimsuited self. I spend a lot of time bouncing between visions of myself, visions of others, imaginations of what could happen. When Wendy S. Walters imagines that the farmhouse woman threw a can of soup at her, that "fiction" allows her to see things she might not have otherwise.

When I "see" myself as if from above, that sitting-in-my-chair-typing self, I see a different perspective. If I look at myself as if I'm a bug on the floor, I see myself differently. If I read this aloud to myself, I hear one voice. If I have an AI bot read it, I hear another. If I write wondering what my writing friends will think of this sentence, I see the writing through one lens. If I imagine my husband or my kids reading it, I am looking through a different one. I call this looking "dissociation," which is a bit of a charged term. Once, at a job interview, someone asked, "Do you mean in the clinical sense?" And I said, "No. Not exactly." But I do think that in order to gain the distance needed to put your story in understandable light, you have to put it into a scene. And that means moving your imagining eye around, getting outside and above yourself. It's not a clinical diagnosis but to achieve this kind of distance, you need to jar your brain from its normal tracks. Metaphors and objects serve to shake up the vision. Letting your mind move from ordinary-length sentences to one incredibly long one, as Miller does, from imagination to fact, as Walters does, or from past to present, as LeMay does, can feel discombobulating, but it can free your writing and your vision.

It's ironic that to achieve this kind of dissociation, you need to let your brain riff associatively. I try to imagine multiple perspectives at a time, letting my brain chase those visions. Sometimes, I read student writing that reminds me of sitting on the bus, next to a very chatty person, who tells me about her relationship to the chair she's sitting on (she once sat on a seat similar to this one when she was visiting her friend Jane, who had cancer, but now she doesn't), her belief about stop signs (why so many? Do we have to stop? What about those cars just running through?) the time she stopped at the store we're passing (hot dogs from 7-Eleven, 99 cents for three), the hat of the guy sitting in front of us (is it beige? Or gray? Or beige gray?). I care about these details because I like my students and I care because people are generally interesting, but her thoughts while riding the bus are not an essay or a story yet. Until she can see me as audience, she can't make me care about the bus situation. It will remain a series of images and thoughts that aren't shaped toward making me see the point of her telling. And, until she sees herself as a character on a bus, explaining to me why she's talking to me, she won't be able to see me, the reader, at all.

Writers live in their heads but that's the problem. No one wants to be in anyone's head for very long. Or in their hearts. They are sad. Empathy is one of the gifts given to you by the experience of moving your perspective around. I understand. I am sad too. They are in love. So am I. They are not sure if this choice was the right one, if their parents were good or bad, if their writing reaches anyone at all. Neither am I. We are sad. We are in love. We are not sure. But that's not quite enough to make your story available to others. We want to feel it like you feel it and this means that you can't be you, writey one, anymore. You have to put yourself in as a narrator on the page if you're going to affect the reader in the way that you are affected. For this to happen, you need distance between yourself author and yourself (as narrator) on the page. Another irony: To bring the reader closer to you, the narrator-entity-on-the-page must step away.

I tell my students, put your body in a place. The idea that they separate the subject (themselves) from the direct object (themselves) begins the process of dissociation. That moving the body around like it's a mannequin on display is the first step in getting the reader to see the narrator as a human. For some reason, telling someone you are sad does not humanize you. It falls flat, emotionless. Who isn't sad? "Get over it. I am sooooo sad," I can hear the junior high school boys mocking.

You cannot feel sorry for yourself. It begins there, with the language. "You could tell I was happy by the way my eyes flipped up toward the ceiling. On the ceiling was the happiness, writ large, like a cupcake. All things good are ceilinged and cupcaked. You cannot tell me differently. I walked to the edge of the kitchen. There is no sadness in corners." Language furthers the effect. The more straightforward and matter of

8. Dissociation versus Distance

fact you tell your story, the more space you create between you narrator and you creator for the reader to fit right in. The readers become snug between the disparate space between the narrator who thinks and narrator who moves their body. The narrator says, "We all want ourselves to be the good guy. But often we are not," But the narrator's body opposes this thought as she carries a kitchen implement across the floor toward her brother. "I still like to think of myself as the picked-on one, even though it was I who, at four, looking at my brother, age two and favorite, walked over to where he was sitting on the floor and hit him over the head with the rolling pin. Not the plastic one."

The reader, with the narrator, believes people want to be good. The reader, in the scene, second-guesses the narrator, wants to put her hand between the narrator's rolling pin and the brother's head while, at the same time, remembers bonking her own little brother on the head for being cuter than her.

You pare back the language. "I opened the car door." Not "I opened the car door of the yellow 1979 Volkswagen Beetle." In the emotion-garnering part of the essay, you don't want super-specific detail, just idiosyncratic detail. "With my pinkie finger in my mouth, muffling what I was trying to say, I told him I was pregnant. I knew if he couldn't really hear me, it wouldn't really be true and we wouldn't have to tell my mother or his mother and in fact the only person that really knew was my finger. My finger, like my fetus, is not a person." Adjectives tell people you're sad about which they have already stipulated they do not care.

The site, as well as the sight, of the body is a catalyst for empathy. What reader doesn't have a body? Make them feel that rolling pin in their hand, that bonk upon the head. Putting distance in between the narrator's thoughts and the narrator's body brings the reader in closer.

But sometimes the writer, in order to get to the narrator, even before she can get to the body, employs more drastic artifice. There are difficult things to talk about, like brothers and pregnancy, and then there are impossible things to talk about, like rape and torture and murder. And for the essay, because the narrator is part of the scene, how they treat the matter is an ethical problem as well as an aesthetic one. How do you put your story on the page so that it communicates to people while still making sure there's room for the reader to breathe, respond, and understand that you, writer, created this art, this artifice, this affect, while still experiencing the actual pain? It can't all be overly aestheticized or it will read as artifice, because then the lyricism is only on the reader—no longer active for the narrator/character/writer. And it can't just be catharsis for the writer, as that's not writing, it's therapy.

Until the dissociation happens, until the writer comes to the blank page and does some writerly work, like position the narrator's body in the glow of the streetlight or put the mom naked on the bed or swirl the sentences like toilet water, I'm not sure where we're going. The point of Gray-Rosendale's book is to explain how dissociation works. It is good for writing, although not necessarily good for healing. She separated from the world. She could see herself. As she sees herself seeing herself, she can understand the dissociation and only then she can stitch herself back into the world. For healing, you must do what Eric LeMay does and bring the narrator, author, and body back together. Preferably while listening to a thunderstorm approach. As Jesmyn Ward positions her of chapters in reverse chronological order, she infuses what she knew about the past with the understanding of who she and her friends became. While tracing her footsteps backward, she can finally examine her brother's death and impart the emotion she felt to the reader. In Brenda Miller's "Swerve," the writer comes in and apologizes for the lightbulbs and the light from the window and the light from the brakes on the car until her piled-up images shine the light back on her. The narrator is transformed because the writer broke completely, at least for a moment, from the narrator. Now, as she returns to the end of the story, she's returned herself to herself.

On the bus, the bus-rider sees the things she passes but she doesn't see herself sitting there talking to me. If she saw herself talking to me, she'd tell me why she's telling me about the hot dogs and how that one time she ate fourteen of them in a row, shoving bun and meat into her face like a postal worker stuffs mail slots, this would be distance which is the first step toward perspective. If then, she started comparing the rigors of bus-riding—the people-watching, the intersection-crossing—to the difficulty of talking to another person on the bus while recounting the difficulty of swallowing that last hot dog and how, and then you saw yourself, on that bus, offering me a hot dog, then you would be dissociating. Then, if you told me "if you really think about it, we are all on the bus all the time, waiting to get off so we can get on another bus and tell that story about how hot dogs and people-watching are the key to happiness," then, you'd be bringing narrator, author, and body back together and would then, be writing her story.

Dissociation and Distance Prompt
This prompt is so straightforward, I hesitate to describe it as such. Writing about a subject in the second- or third-person point of view

provides immediate distance. I also think it makes us contemplate what happens with syntax, rhythm, interiority, and word choice when writing fiction and nonfiction. By transforming the point of view of this paragraph from first to third, does it necessarily read like fiction? What continues to root this paragraph from above in nonfiction, although I've changed the POV?

> She lies on the bed with Zoë who is asleep. She smells her hair. "It's because I'm her mom that I can do this. I can stroke her arm. I can kiss her neck. There is a reason I can do this," she justifies. She's her mom. But that thought makes her dissociate. She hovers above and sees her lips kissing Zoë's cheek and it looks weird: too intimate. She scoots over, moves away. Was this moving away the beginning of the gap? Was it her own nervousness that the gap between them was space too much for someone else to move in and make Zoë's body familiar? Zoë's familiar body was hers, cultivated by her. But someone else will find it wild and want to make it theirs. She would have done anything if Zoẽ would stay three years old and under the crook of her arm forever, but her arm begins to cramp, and Zoe's head itches and they both start talking about their favorite foods and get hungry and have to get up. Bodies usually win these arguments.
>
> (149)[9]

Besides having to manage a lot of repeated "her"s, replacing them with "Zoë's", I changed the conditional "woulds" to straightforward past tense, since the third-person POV did enough distancing. I think this version makes the scene a little more creepy. It also might call for more explanation. From the first-person point of view, we understand the gap between their bodies must eventually separate, which is where newcomer-bodies come in. But in the third person, the mom already feels separate.

By playing with first, second, and third points of view, you, the writer, are in charge of the distance of the lens. You may be able to write some hard stuff that you've avoided. You might notice that interiority is easier in the first person. It might be better to make scenes using the third. And the second person might allow a kind of lyricism and intimacy not as available in the second or third. By practicing in all three, you learn how to control the camera lens, zooming in, zooming out so the reader can envision the experience and you can detail it with measured focus. And you also may learn to drop the camera for a bit and find that first-person voice closes the distance between reader and writer.

Notes

1 Brenda Miller, "Lions and Tigers and Bears, Oh My! On Courage in Creative Nonfiction," *Bending Genre*, 2nd ed., Bloomsbury Publishing (2023).
2 Laura Gray-Rosendale, *College Girl*, Excelsior Editions (2013).
3 Nicole Walker, *Processed Meats*, Torrey House Press (2021).
4 Ibid.
5 Nicole Walker, *Sustainability: A Love Story*, Ohio University Press (2018).
6 Brenda Miller, "Swerve," *Brevity Magazine*, https://brevitymag.com/nonfiction/swerve/ (2009).
7 Ibid.
8 Eric LeMay, *In Praise of Nothing: Essays, Memoir, and Experiments*, Emergency Press (2014).
9 Walker, *Processed Meats*.

Chapter 9

FINDING THE MUSIC

Writing is hard. Writing about personal hard stuff is extra-hard. Writing about the natural world, its beauty and its destruction, makes that hard writing meaningful to me. I'm not a religious person, but I am a person deeply in love with the world. When writing or getting that writing into the world becomes too difficult, I remind myself to increase the available reality by making connections between unlike things to broaden the imagination, heck, to even make connections between like things because we have much in common with the things and beings of the world.

Sometimes, it feels very quiet out there. The hard thing is too hard. All you hear are echoes of something lost. Or the retreating footsteps of something you're in the process of losing. You hear about the deaths out there, over there, at the school, with its shootings, and the only noise you make is a guttural sound in the bottom of your throat. Sometimes it's hard to believe in anything. Sometimes, it's impossible to believe that anything you have to say on the subject is weak or floundering or one a billion voices crying "no" and no God with ears big enough to listen.

Screaming at the television news, lying on the floor in a fetal position, staring out the window to see if maybe Winged Victory might fly by, seem like an appropriate response to absence, loss, grief, the gaping abyss. Perhaps one of the gentler ways to re-enter the world is to deepen your attention to it. You may not be able to write directly about the news, the shooting, the God, or the horror. By writing tangentially to the hard thing, by delving into research about algae, or by studying the grasshopper chewing on the leaf of your Swiss chard, you start to fill in that abyss with the soil of your investigations. Each adjective, verb, noun, preposition builds a rope around which you can wrap your hands and begin to climb out of that black hole. You might not be able to fly out of there, but maybe, you'll begin to sing.

The world is a pretty big place. We can't wrap our hands around it, let alone our heads. How can we save something we can't fully imagine? Plus, we humans, in our great God complex, are the ones who broke the planet.

Maybe we're not the best choice to try to put it back together. Instead, maybe we should continue to shatter it. Break it into its constituent parts. Perhaps we should shine our big fluorescent imaginations onto every living and non-living thing. Highlight it. Make it numinous. Maybe it's through the shattering we can see the way toward some sort of saving—of ourselves. Of our planet. For everything that is accounted is made present. And the more presence accounted for, the more planet there is.

About appreciating every tiny thing in the world, John Muir wrote

> The universe would be incomplete without man; but it would also be incomplete without the smallest transmicroscopic creature that dwells beyond our conceitful eyes and knowledge ... The fearfully good, the orthodox, of this laborious patchwork of modern civilization cry "Heresy" on every one whose sympathies reach a single hair's breadth beyond the boundary epidermis of our own species. Not content with taking all of earth, they also claim the celestial country as the only ones who possess the kind of souls for which that imponderable empire was planned.
>
> (283)[1]

Poets may be empire builders too. But they do a good job of looking at things a single hair's breadth in size. Poets focus on the tiniest details like blades of grass, the barbules of raven feathers, the flake of aspen bark. It is from these tiny things that patterns, systems, habits, and metaphors emerge. Poets work their way to the big picture through the tiny things, illuminating the smallest of beings, making big connections on their way, knitting together an understanding of how the microscopic concatenate—and maybe understanding is the first step in saving the environment, or learning how to not make it worse. Perhaps, instead of burning it all down, we can sit down, and count, describe, embrace, and illuminate the objects of the world.

W. S. Merwin's poem, "A Scale in May," is political. It's a call to action. It's also a method for how to write. And to live. Listen to Merwin take count of the details, enlarging the world as he goes:

> Now all my teachers are dead except silence   **I am trying to read what the five poplars are writing   on the void**   Of all the beasts to man alone death brings justice   But I desire   To kneel in a doorway empty except for the song   Who made time provided also its fools   Strapped in watches and with ballots for their choices   Crossing the frontiers of invisible kingdoms   To succeed

consider what is as though it were past Deem yourself inevitable and take credit for it **If you find you no longer believe enlarge the temple** Through the day the nameless stars keep passing the door That have come all that way out of death Without questions   The walls of light shudder and an owl wakes in the heart   I cannot call upon words   The sun goes away to set elsewhere   Before nightfall colorless petals blow under the door   And the shadows Recall their ancestors in the house beyond death   At the end of its procession through the snow   Falling the water remembers to laugh[2]

The poplars are writing. Look at their bark. Decipher the message. How do you enlarge the temple? Connect the dots. What dots? The pixels. The hyphae. You can't connect if you haven't counted them. Highlight them. Writing illuminates the dots. It finds the objects of the universe, shines on them, and then goes deeper in. "Wall of light shudders and an owl wakes in the heart."

Ballots. Petals. Pixels. When you feel stuck either by discomfort or uncertainty, spend a few seconds thinking about a key sensory detail. Free-associate on the detail. What does it remind you of? Can you remember seeing something similar in the past? What are its qualities—shape, color, size? Does that spark analogy? If you had to tell these details of your own story, what would they invent for that detail? The detail will begin to scoop up significant linkages, and these may provide a way for the story to move forward in a new, surprising direction. Instead of telling the story in a straightforward way, the author amasses material, metaphor, and connections, adding texture and depth and providing multiple ideas to exist at once and offer multiple entrees into the story.

The more dots you can see, the more dots there are. The writer goes inside the stamen of a flower, finds the whiskers on a bee. It makes paper out of birch skin and pink out of dianthus. It slows the hummingbird's wings and brings close the barnacle above a humpback whale's eye. So much stuff of this world. If you find you don't believe: Enlarge the Temple. Make the world bigger by seeing more stuff even if that stuff is more human cells. Make the world bigger by making room for other points of view.

Working with Teacher-Fellows from the Diné Institute at my university has shown me other ways to increase the available universe. Stories about the burial place of placenta rooting the author to place, stories about cutting juniper trees to patch the roof of the shade house, respecting the haggard-looking sage plant enough to say to it, "Hey, I'll go look for another sage, you look like you've given enough lately," were new to me. Although I lead the seminar, these writers lead me to see ground and trees and sage brush in wild shades of green. There was a non-hierarchical connection for these writers. The bushes, the work of tree cutting, the respect for the needs of the sage plant: These relationships felt like they were horizontal, that humans shared the same plane as these plants with equanimity, like a partnership.

Making connections with the stuff of this world doesn't just stave off loneliness. It subverts the kind of thinking that humans are the center of the universe or the top of the food chain. This hierarchy may have given us a sense of superiority, but it also comes with the risk that it's a long fall from the top. You're likely to crater. When the center gives way, the black hole consumes everything. But, if you, human, are just one entity among a web of connections, then if someone needs you, they'll give you a little tug. If you need something, you can pull a little bit of energy and support from the web of connections that holds you. Writers, by making connections through metaphor, through form, by putting their narrator's and character's bodies in a place, help us see the connections. The words "like" or "as" in the simile are links that connect one to one to one.

Some environmentalist writers imagine paying deep attention as a kind of political action. Donna Haraway, in her book *Staying with the Trouble, Making Kin in the Chthulucene,* writes about kinship between humans and all the things in the world. If enlarging the temple has a religiosity about it, Haraway's enlarging is the world wide web—but the ecological, not the computer, version. All the paths in the woods made by the ants, the squirrels, the fungi, the coyote, the tree roots converge, diverge, and converge again.

In non-Western cultures, the path that moves forward like a road, pushing toward some destination, isn't the only narrative model. Instead of a train track or a freeway or even a path in the woods, some cultures hang their narrative structures on different images. Navajo storytellers consider rain, spiderwebs, and spirals as possible models instead of the usual track or arc. Haraway's *Staying with the Trouble* spells out an argument that to stave off the worst effects of climate change, we'll have to change the way we think. Doing so will require us to change the way we narrate our lives. Early in the book, she considers the string game Cat's Cradle and what it means for Navajo story-making.

> In the Navajo language, string games are called na'atl'o . . . these string figures are thinking as well as making practices, pedagogical practices

and cosmological performances. Some Navajo thinkers describe string games as one kind of patterning for hózhó, a term imperfectly translated in English as "harmony," "beauty," "order," and right relations with the world," including right relations of humans and nonhumans.

(13)[3]

Haraway considers what might be possible if we think using different frameworks, languages, and contexts from our conventional ones. Perhaps then we could see different ways of restoring balance to the world. The difference, to my mind, between paths or roads and rain or nests or spiderwebs is that the way may not be made only by racing from point a to point b on a straightforward narrative trail. Connections are made by junctures, stretches, tugs, diversions, and detours. Conjunctions like *and* build this webby world. The prepositions *between*, *with*, *through*, and *near* shape the network. As Haraway says, "Not *in* the world but *of* the world, that crucial difference in English prepositions is what leads me to weave Navajo string figures" (14)[4].

These prepositions matter. Staying *with* the trouble is not the same as staying *in* trouble. One of the worst ways I responded to the sexual interference was trying to move past it, pretend it wasn't that big of a deal, trying whatever I could to make everything all right. I do that now—gloss over the hard things. If I really did go wrong somewhere, it is there. I brushed it off as not a big deal. I wrote over it. I wrapped it into a narrative of, well, shit happens. I'll do anything to "make things fine." Donna Haraway's advice to stay with the trouble is good for not only climate change, but for other kinds of trauma. It's the root of healing— don't just glide on by. Stay and let it sink in. We don't want to sit with climate change any more than we want to sit with childhood sex trouble. But maybe if we stay and look at how messed up it really is, we'd realize we have a lot of work to do. Again, the strategies in this book are meant to help you stay with the trouble and yet not let it consume you like a black hole. The creative work to make braided essays, or find an object that supplies a lens, or how to switch your perspective so you can see the story differently, or to pull sward from ground to find the dirt, the worm, the grass, and the root all tucked together, makes more reality every second you look.

Peter Friederici's recent book *Beyond Climate Breakdown: Envisioning New Stories of Radical Hope* argues that climate narrative doesn't need to be a tragic one—one where we ride down unbending, story-limiting, option delineating railroad tracks. Instead, he writes,

What we need, then, is not to discard narrative but to reclaim it from the dominance of the relative handful of narrators whose dead-end story lines have taken us to the brink of catastrophe. We need to expand the world's narrative, the human story, from a few inflexible strings of meaning into a woven tapestry of far more threads... We need to broaden it so that it encompasses the full complexity of relationships between humans and the more-than-human, the world of plants and animals and weather and climate cycles that is increasingly reclaiming its place as actor. And we need to broaden it so that it contains within the voices of far more people of far more cultures that have so far been represented in mainstream discourse and decision-making.

(135)[5]

Broadening the story and shifting perspectives underpin the craft strategies I've outlined in this book. Being able to see your story in relation to other elements means that sometimes your story is big, sometimes above as if from a streetlight, sometimes full of meaning, sometimes ordinary. Sometimes your story is the grass, the root, the dirt, or the worm. Sometimes it's the whole layer of sward whose prairie roots go incredibly deep. These perspective shifts offer ways to shape your story. They also help us shift the common paradigm from one that conceives that the planet exists for humans to consume its resources, to one where humans are members of a shared planet. Haraway's conceit for how we see the universe provides a way to "see" the world differently, a way to write it with more reality, a way to hear all the voices, not just the loudest, and not just the human.

It takes creative effort to shift these perspectives. It takes energy to connect idea to idea. It takes a big leap of faith to enlarge the temple—to make our eyes see more. But imagination is the best tool we've got. If we're stuck in a black hole physically, we're stuck. But if we're trapped in a black hole *psychically*, we have the creative oomph to propel ourselves out of there. Imaginative writing, whether fiction, poetry, nonfiction, playwriting, or all of the above, provides not only a ladder to climb out of the black hole but the ground upon which to set the ladder. Use all the tools and genres you've got to make it back into starlight.

The hardest times to live through are the hardest times to write about. Trying to balance how much of an impact the hard thing made upon you with the fact that you're probably writing in a more ordinary time to an ordinary person means you might have to employ hybrid strategies. While writing *How to Plant a Billion Trees*, at times I had to leap into a kind of fiction, an imagined space, to express how hard a breakup with my boyfriend of five years hit me. Like other sections of the manuscript, where writing the hard stuff in mimetic representational style seemed impossible, I took the opportunity to make the story bigger both by adding metaphors and stretching the bounds of imagination to show *how* I was feeling when the event was going down. Here, birds, trees, and chickens don't stand in for the narrator or her boyfriend. Instead, they become the narrator's escape hatch. She can't bear the moment, so she imagines something more fanciful than what happened. Perhaps such imaginings made it possible to understand that hard place and why it made such an impact on my psyche.

> "I cannot eat chicken for the rest of my life. I need something else. I'm going to move to Hawaii. Or to Singapore with Rashimi." My boyfriend, soon ex, walked up to me, put his hand on my stomach, and said, "I could have conjured a baby there."
>
> "Look. You did say we could have a baby. You changed your mind about that. But no. Don't conjure. I can't have a baby upside down. It's contraindicated." I said as I edged myself onto the strong-enough branch, my knees pinching its curve.
>
> "We were going to have a baby but now I realize that babies are a bad idea. They are the antithesis of progress. I am going to become something else," I wished I had said.
>
> "Once a tree, always a tree," I swung down like I used to in grade school before the babysitter, before I wore make-up, before I thought needed a man-like creature to navigate the path for me.
>
> "I would like to be a bird. A bird without any babies." I imagined I said.
>
> "I'm 24 now. My dad will die in two years. You and I will actually succeed in getting back together and then falling apart again. You will tell me I'm fucked up and that I need to deal with my father issues and I will say that sounds a lot like psychotherapy to me. You'll say let's quit smoking and I'll say OK and then I'll say fuck that and I think that maybe you leave me finally for the final time because I'm too flexible. Watch me rise up and grab this branch. I can throw myself from this tree like a gymnast. Is it sexy or do I look like a pre-teen—short, square, smoking behind your back while I wonder where my doll Amber went?" The world looked upside down from there, but whether that was before or after the leap, no one could have said.

After he moved out of our duplex, I went upside down anyway. I lost my mind. I drove by Drew's apartment. I walked by his work. Stalker like. I managed to find myself at the same gay bar watching the same drag show. I over-identified with Bonnie Tyler's *Total Eclipse of the Heart* and bit Drew's ear when the man in the blue gown and long eyelashes sang, "Turn around, Bright Eyes." I lost 20 pounds. I drank gin martinis without vermouth or olives.

I rely on innate optimism. I don't know where it comes from. It's different from hope. Hope requires evidence. Optimism is foolish. It leads to disappointment. But, when I crawl on the forest floor, looking under a fallen log for mushrooms, certain that I will find a chanterelle there, I can't help but feel like even I do not find an orange, crenellated cap rising in the moss, a sun lifting its sky, there will be another one under the next tree.

I believe there will always be one more tree to look under.

I believe that if I root around in the dirt of my own story, I'll find the parts of me that had been discombobulated by the babysitter and rearrange them in a manner that makes me an feel like an regular, organized human.

Rachel Louise Snyder in *Women We Buried, Women We Burned* writes that after her mother's funeral, she returned to her third grade classroom. The room was silent. Like everyone but her was in on the joke. Everyone knew her heart-story: her mom was dead. She was on the outside of the forest, looking in. As she wrote about how she saw herself in relationship to others, she began to see how alienation has dogged her throughout her life. Theresa Mailhot writes in *Heart Berries* of her troubled upbringing, her mental health diagnoses, her father's murder, and her partner's unreliability that only through writing was she able to re-organize and understand her trauma. Mailhot's distance is two-fold: writing about these hard things is one level of distance. Writing about writing it is another. With that second layer of distance, Mailhot could see how writing about writing gave her agency over her story. Melissa Febos in *Girlhood* recounts how her early-developed body alienated her from both the girls and boys in her grade, which made her different—both stronger and stranger. But in writing about it, she sees through the lens of our cultural sexism, she can now appreciate, through her writing, that that strength and strangeness gave her charged observation skills and unique perspective. Roxane Gay's *Hunger* explains how her rape disconnected her mind from her body. By writing, she began to draw her mind and body back together, ounce by detailed ounce. Gay expands the available reality by letting us see into her most intimate relationship—that with her body—and sharing it with us. By writing, these authors not only stitched themselves into a more supportive, substantial world, but they also wrote what they saw from the outside into that fabric.

Difficult stories bring some subjects into specific relief. By zoning in on all the details, a writer can make a specific moment last longer, make the small seem large, exaggerate the senses so that the reader experiences that story as something beyond the ordinary scope of things. If you stay with the trouble, be it climate change or personal trauma, details you didn't see reveal themselves. It's not that the trouble is necessarily fixable—it's that by staying and looking, you may find some of the complex connections between the things of the world. How do you climb out of the hole? You make the world bigger by pulling sand, grain by grain, into your hole until you're level again with the surface of the world. You look at the world closely, through a microscope, through a telescope, upside down and, if you're gentle, inside-out.

To repeat the lines from Merwin's poem, "If you find you no longer believe, enlarge the temple." These words encourage writers to elevate all they observe, to imagine with all their senses. While the hard stuff doesn't go away, it becomes less bulky and intrusive when there is so much else to write about. By paying attention to all the available realities, the tiny details, the writer balances that dark, difficult moment with an abundance of life. For example, Geetha Iyer writes intricately about a Panamanian frog in such exquisite detail that our thoughts are saturated with its presence, even as we learn the frog is threatened.

> A dark, speckled frog the size of a walnut climbs a guayacán tree that rises thirty meters from the ground. Its target is the stumpy scar of a large branch that fell off many years ago, which was then hollowed by termites, toucans, and fungal rot. With the start of the rain season, the cavity is likely to fill with water, a miniature marsh suited to the frog's miniature needs. Precarious though the journey may be, the frog will go to great lengths and heights in search of any such small hollows. It finds them in the forest canopy within the throats of bromeliad plants, in tree holes and broken bamboo stems. It finds them in the bountiful litter of the forest floor, in halved fruit husks and emptied seed pods, and the boat-like hollows of fallen palm fronds.

> For a creature so small, the frog hops and climbs with seemingly inexhaustible gumption. It has the enviable advantage of being

toxic—the consequence of a diet of ants, mites, small beetles and other arthropods—a fact advertised by its patterning, a muddy brown speckled with mint green dots. Animals learn from prior association that this is a creature that tastes like numbing and nausea, muscle spasms and death. Would-be predators spit, retch, foam at the mouth, and don't try to swallow again.

Nonetheless, the frog travels with caution. It emerges from the forest edge onto a weedy lawn. It freezes at suggestions of danger—swooping birds, naïve cats, a car backing out of a garage. Now it climbs flowerpots and patio furniture. It scales a metal fence post, falls off and tries again. It sits awhile in a dimple in an uneven concrete patio, which sometimes fills with backsplash off the tin roof overhead. It perches on the rim of a disregarded, rusting bean can and looks within—water prickling with telltale signs of activity, mosquito larvae sipping air through siphons that they poke through the water's surface.[6]

Iyer travels at the pace of the frog. At the eye-level of the frog. Iyer is the frog, the predator, the narrator, the dangers. This essay gets at the hard subjects of superabundance and threat, made environments sitting next to natural ones. It's hard to convey the import of these tiny poison dart frogs. Geetha does it by letting not one detail go.

Wallace Stevens' edict that one should write "No ideas about the thing but the thing itself" sidesteps the problem of pesky ideas getting into our poems. The ideas are already in the thing—the thing is merely microscopic. What we need to see already exists. We just need to be look harder. Just listen to all the stories of all the beings of the universe, the poets say. Our attention is all we can give the universe. "Attention, taken to its highest degree, is the same thing as prayer. It presupposes faith and love," Simone Weil wrote. Bright green pine needles sparking chlorophyll towards the sun make a different sound than duff-colored pine needles, fallen to the forest floor. Those make a sound even the microbes can hear. But still, if you're patient enough, you can hear that slow stretching into the next sound.

Brian Doyle's short essay after the September 11th attack "Leap" does this beauty-writing carefully. As he writes the first and last names of witnesses who watched people jump from the Twin Towers, he repeats their names. He repeats the phrase "pink mist everywhere," which normally refers to sun setting over oceans or the breath of morning particulating over red canyon rocks. In "Leap," Doyle means bodies exploding on the ground. He is not aestheticizing these deaths. The tone is matter of fact, journalistic, but the repetition incants the darkness that brought us to this place. There were real witnesses with first and last names. There were real jumpers with first and last names that we will never decipher because they have become particulated into pink mist. He isn't making them pretty. He's making them beautiful. He's making them as hard core real as he can. He's making them meaningful.

Brian Doyle took one of the hardest stories to happen to our country in recent memory and made it as real and a hard as it could be, nearly invoking us to stand up and imagine taking one, two, three steps toward the edge of a burning building, then reaching out for someone's hand and leaping off. He increases the available reality not only by keenly observing each second of the moment the pair jump from the building, but he also adds something to the story. Through the repetition, the points of view of the people below, the sonic beat of the last lines, he's able, without sentimentality, to land on the idea of hope. To take the blackest ash of devastation and see somewhere inside a spark of light is the definition of enlarging the temple.

Sometimes, I've found that writing the hard stuff plainly and with certainty creates a space for the reader to fill with their emotion. Instead of telling a reader how you felt, you lay it out for them almost mechanically so that the facts hit starkly, like staccato piano notes. Conversely, addressing the reader or a particular person directly can create intimacy. The reader feels the author whispering a secret to them. For example, Kiese Laymon's memoir *Heavy* is written ostensibly to his mother, but the reader acquires the purview of the you—the special position that only true intimacy would allow. Early in the book, he writes to his mother,

> I remember you making me take my clothes off and lie across the same bed we used to sleep in. I don't think I've ever screamed like that. You made me put my face down into the bed so I couldn't brace myself. As much as the lashes hurt, knowing you were beating me at nine years old as hard as you could while looking at my fat naked body hurt way more. The tearing of flesh hurt less than it should have, I think, because I knew you didn't really want to hurt me.
>
> (46)[7]

The "you" here works in complicated ways—replaying the scene so that the mother must remember, letting the reader in on the intimacy of the you, which feels awkward, like we're eavesdropping on something supremely personal, and a "you" that condemns reader, mother, and narrator alike—this is what you've driven me to, the text seems to say. For you to understand what it was like to be an overweight, Black kid, you're going to have to get naked on the bed with me. Laymon's use of the second person creates a swirl of emotions that the reader spends the rest of the book trying to figure out how to feel. This wildly intimate voice catapulted his story into novel critical and artistic realms. How did he make that voice work so well and so consistently?

Often, developing one's characteristic voice comes during revision. One of the great things about revision, the fact that it can be a painful process notwithstanding, is that you can make messy drafts, write too close to the bone, or too far from it, and then go back and revise it. I think writers tend to be resilient people. If things break in real life, as they often do in writing, they have great faith in their ability to fix it. I'll recount stories of writers I know who have succeeded in fixing things despite the odds, both in their writing and in real life.

Natalie Diaz, when visiting my university to give a reading, told the audience that when you revise, add material before you delete or subtract anything. As one of the premises of this text is to encourage writers to expand the available reality, this advice comports with Diaz's. In adding metaphor, associations, objects, shifts in points of view and so on, revision becomes not a matter of cutting and deleting but about layering, embedding, deepening, and adding texture.

The hard stuff sometimes feels hard, matter-of-fact; perhaps a John Stuart Mill would describe it as nasty, brutish, and short. The act of writing might not soften those hard things, but it can let hard things be a catalyst via which they connect with other stories, other perspectives, other people. The more material in a story, the more available reality, the more doors through which readers can enter the text. The more the story resonates with the stuff of our world, the more it resonates with the reader. The writer, by their generous sharing, makes the hard thing less a nugget of an island and helps find its continental comrades, be they story, turtle, egg, or human.

Sometimes it's easier to hear your voice through other people's lips. In Czerwiec's *Crafting the Lyric Essay,* she again attends to "Fish" with such kindness and care. Hearing is an inherent part of reading, and Heidi reads this essay with generous acuity.

> Here, 'current' evokes both the increased pressure of the dammed river and the electricity and both echoed I the 'cables of fire streaming.' The play on 'hard row to hoe' gets presented as the sonic and eye

rhyme of 'All the roe she had to hoe.' Like the salmon funneled to climb the fish ladder, 'Eggs lined up in her tubes ... Follicular. Funicular.' The exact rhyme ad syllabic stress, as well as the wordplay of those two words, emphasize both ethe reproductive drive of, etymologically, eggs lined up, but also suggest the folly of this funneling of the salmon on the ladder. The 'red roe' become 'little apples,' the 'apple of her eye' that drives her maternal instinct, and the reddish speckled appearance her 'apple-skin' takes on at this reproductive stage of ripening.' And yet the loving 'polishing' of those egg-apples becomes the 'water polishing the concrete' to a fluid, unstressed slipperiness, to a no-no-no nothing hard step-stresses that are negated, hastening her death.

(78)[8]

It's clear, I suspect, that both Heidi and I began as poets. In fact, we studied under Jacqueline Osherow, Donald Revell and guest writer Elinor Wilner in graduate school. Our ears were literally honed by Jackie. I'm surprised we don't look like elves, she shaped them so sharp.

Natalie Diaz's poem "They Don't Love You Like I Love You," riffs from a song written by the Yeah Yeah Yeahs, called *Maps*, which Beyoncé covered, does the great work of making connections between bands and poets, but also opens the text of the song to allow entry of Diaz's own words, making this poem a new thing—now not only about romantic love but also about motherly love and territory and stolen lands and broken promises. She repeats the lines from the song, writing them in italics, and then seems to answer them with images less lilting and soft. The lines in regular font insist, state, and bring the title of the song, maps, back into the lyrics of the poem, even though neither the Yeah Yeah Yeahs nor Beyoncé ever sing the word "map" in their versions of the song.

I'll say, say, say,
I'll say, say, say,
What is the United States if not a clot

of clouds? If not spilled milk? Or blood?
If not the place we once were
in the millions? America is *Maps*—

(17)[9]

Now look how much more material she made extant in the world. To pull lines from a song into another form not only lets the poem spin the words in another direction, but it also recasts the song itself as now we hear Diaz's voice singing alongside Beyoncé's and the Yeah Yeah Yeahs'.

Marrying writing with music reminds us where songs began. One of my favorite essays, reprinted in John D'Agata's *The Next American Essay*, is Susan Mitchell's lyric essay "Notes Toward a History of Scaffolding." This essay, she unpacks the word "scaffold," discusses the history of art, reimagines manuscripts from the Middle Ages, and watches, from her hotel room, the scaffolding being erected by the workers who are refurbishing the hotel, and remembers a different time and place, Boca Raton, Florida (June 17), where she watched a bird fledge. In this piece, words for nest equal words for scaffold. And, when she gets to the part about essays leaning upon the etymology, history, image, and scene, she finds a baby bird who launches from the nest.

> I actually saw it happen. A bird falling from the roof of a building. The bird let out a little cry as it dropped—one story, two—then, just as if it had hit something solid in the air, it bounced into flight. Hardly back on the roof, it was falling again, and falling, letting out that cry. But were the falls failed attempts at flight? The bird seemed to be throwing itself off the roof—falling on purpose. Out of the plunge perfected, flight pushed up as necessity. There was thrust behind it—the fear of falling. And with each practice fall, the cry lasted longer until the cry became a run of notes, a flutter along the avifaunal scale. Out of the fall, the cry shivered up and down, the natural embodiment of thrill. Suddenly, I understood. The bird wasn't practicing flight. It knew how to fly. The bird was teaching itself to sing.
>
> (239)[10]

Mitchell's epiphany embodies the premise of this book. Writing is falling. Catching oneself. Revising. Flinging oneself into the pit again. Rising up. Until finally one gets the hang of it and learns how to sing.

In *Crafting the Lyric Essay*, Czerwiec performs her own lyrical riffs in a short, resonant essay called "Resonance." She pulls phrases from other authors to whom she nods in a footnote, This essay contains riffs/reworkings of Lia Purpura's "Autopsy Report,'" Jamaica Kincaid's "Girl," Wallace Stevens' "Thirteen Ways of Looking at a Blackbird," Timothy O'Brien's "The Things They Carried," Shakespeare's *Midsummer Night's Dream*, and Brian Doyle's "Leap," and borrows its form from John Scalzi's "Being Poor." The essay begins,

9. Finding the Music

I shall write about resonance. Here's the truth: when I first heard the resonance, I sang out loud. The song burst forth; I could not stop it. And now that I've admitted singing, I shall admit this: what sounded forth was jubilant, rhapsodic, astounding—whatever is the opposite of calm.

Resonance is what Judith Kitchen insists with her declaration against D'Agata: "to be lyric there must be a lyre. . . . The lyre, not the liar."

Resonance of origins, lyric, Orphic, endorphic. Strike a chord, and accord of notes, denoting and connoting, a word-chord of wordplay, proliferating.

This is how to begin. This is how to begin again. This is how to wear your refrain with a difference. Don't space your rhymes too far apart for the ear to hear. Don't amplify your alliteration, lest you write like the slut you are so bent on becoming.

(81)[11]

I want to retype the entire essay here for what it demonstrates—all the lyric power that you can summon by using repetition, alliteration, rhyme, and all the power it gets from repurposing other sources. Not only do those other sources fill the content of the piece, but they also provide its structure. By organizing the fragments to her purpose, Czerwiec's rhythmic sentences thrum, both example and explanation of how music and leaning on words we know well, l ike the part from Jamaica Kincaid's *Girl* "like the slut you are so bent on becoming," and Judith Kitchen's wordplay, "lyre, not the liar." The reality that already existed is pulled up and into service, recharging the original text and singing the new. Hence the title and the repeated word doing the work it says it will, resonating between old and new, lip and ear.

Drawing up and on other texts and media constructs a web again—something parallel to the web of connections between humans and all beings on the planet. This web is also a library of all music, film, books, and art. Well, this web is also like our internet's world wide web. But unlike the digital version, instead of just seeing what art exists, the work spins another thread.

Bhanu Kapil's *Humanimal: A Project for Future Children* begins with the note

This work is based upon the true story of Kamala and Amala, two girls found living with wolves in Bengal, India in 1920. My source text, the diary of an Indian missionary, Reverend Joseph Singh, was first published in 1945 as a companion text to *Wolf-Children and Feral Man*, a book of essays by the Denver anthropologist Robert Zingg. In the jungle, on a Mission to convert the tribal population, Singh had heard stories of 'two white ghosts' roaming with a mother wolf and her pack of cubs. He decided to track them. Upon discovering the 'terrible creatures,' to be human, he killed the wolves and brought the children back to his church-run orphanage, the Home, in Midnapure. For the next decade, he documented his attempt to teach the girls language, upright movement, and a moral life. Despite his efforts, Amala died within a year of capture, of nephritis. Kamala lived to be about sixteen, when she died of TB (IX-X).[12]

I can't imagine such a gift of a found text. It's an ideal vehicle to expound upon colonization. I would love to know these girls and their animal bonds. This seems like an ideal subject to think about hierarchies and webs of knowledge and notions of morality. But this is not a text meant for me to interrogate. It's for Kapil, who enlarges the history of what was known into a resonant form of what could be. A few lines from her interpretation, her extension, her re-visioning:

> As if from the wolf-girl's perspective: The Cook fed us meats of many kinds. I joined my belly to the belly of the next girl. It was pink and we opened our beaks for meat. It was wet and we licked the dictionary off each other's faces.
>
> (14)[13]

Of this story, many texts came—films and histories and monographs. But Kapil's version is hers alone. How do you wrench emotion from a hundred-year-old story? Bring in the details (check out the kite rope). Bring in the animals. Bring in your own family.

Of the sixteen children who were born, only seven—six boys and a girl—survived into childhood proper. One of the boys pushed the girl off the roof and then there were six. My father was the second oldest, and though I not sure if the image—my aunt Subudhra falling upside down to her death, a kite's slim rope still bound to her wrist wrapped twice around her knuckles—is relevant to the story I am telling, it accompanies it. In the quick, black take of a body's flight, a body's eviction or sudden loss of place, the memory of descent functions as a subliminal flash.[14]

Combine that dark narrative of one girl who died within a year of being separated from her wolf family with the girl who died eight years later, who howled for her sister. Add a trickle of paternalism. Layer that with a band of physical abuse. Press those layers together in memory's time-lapse. Let them sit for a few years.

Start digging. Start writing.

- Writing the hard stuff is a bit like juggling multiple balls.
- Reach deep into your emotions.
- Step back and put the narrator on the page.
- Research your own stuff.
- Research information completely tangential to your stuff.
- Write with assonance. Consonance. Resonance.
- Get thee to a nunnery so you can find metaphors in the gardens, the naves, the shared pews, the kitchen.
- Make those sentences shorter. Longer.
- Where did I put my object lesson anyway?

As was the case when Brenda Miller described in her essay "Lions and Tigers and Bears Oh My! Courage in Nonfiction" as she read aloud from her essay, she hadn't thought that she'd been being brave. When she wrote the essay, she hadn't felt the sadness she described. She was too busy honing her sentences, which is one reason writing the hard stuff isn't necessarily retraumatizing. But, even as she honed, she accessed. She found a way to get to the emotion, which is why, after she read the piece out loud, the audience called her brave. She brought the emotion to the table, even if she herself wasn't feeling the emotion in that moment.

How do we get there? When I was writing about when my mom found out about the babysitter or discovered I was pregnant, how did I access what that moment felt like?

Often, I could access the scene: I remembered sitting on the piano, telling the babysitter I was pregnant, but I could not for the life of me remember how I felt. Except I felt stupid. Stupid is a kind of garbage. How did I stay with the trouble for the whole book? By looking for trouble elsewhere: in the forests outside of Portland, in the freezer where I kept chicken to make for my not-ready-to-be-married boyfriend, in the science of mycorrhizal fungi, in the promise of trees, after devastating fire coming back. How did all this trouble not sink me into a black hole of loss? I kept it moving.

Scene can set the stage for emotion, but it can't *be* the emotion. The emotion has to come from voice—from the depth of what you know to be true to the cadence of your actual vocal cords. And voice here can draw from the lessons of the lyric. In music, minor chords suggest sadness. A minor chord contains a flat note. In the C major scale, the notes are C, E and G. After finding these notes, simply move the third note (the E) down by one fret, which creates a note called a lowered or flat third. *BBC's Science Focus* discusses the neurological underpinning that may explain why minor notes create that feeling of sadness, "Back in the 19th century, German scientist Hermann von Helmholtz showed that minor chords create more complex sound waves, which are less harmonious and less comfortable to process."[15]

How can language create that same sense of melancholy? I take a clue from words less harmonious and less comfortable. In a scene from *How to Plant a Billion Trees,* when I begin to put together the idea that my body is connected not only to trauma, but also to action and to the earth, a less dire emotion begins to emerge. I jump between scenes and memories, details from the distant past and from fungi science. I move from body of plant to body of human. My body. This earth.

> Water lets us see everything differently. A wet pine needle—divining rod, drinking straw, kaleidoscope pulls different metaphors from it than a dry one—accusing finger, magician's wand, firestarter— does. I've seen different trees on different continents. I have held lamb's ear to my cheek and unticked kernels from wild wheat. I have picked mushrooms in deserts and rainforests--shrimpers, little brown jobbers, milk caps, amanita muscaria, chanterelles, boletes, lobsters. The forest floor bursts with babies. The mother mycorrhizae lay underground, stretches on her back, and waits for the water to tickle her into birth.
>
> I walked in the duff. I must have millions of spores stuck to my feet. I walked along the Great Salt Lake and in the field behind my house before the Mormon Church was built. I walked across the street to the babysitter's house. I walked up the stairs to the women's clinic. I walked to Chadbourne Lane and I walked to Stansbury Lake where I put my spore-covered feet on the board of a windsurfer and made it halfway across the lake.

As the producer of the text, I don't know for sure if this paragraph conveys the emotion I want to convey, but I hope it does. To arrive at the syntax of this moment isn't all a matter of machine-like thinking, though. You have to get there, somehow. Or does the syntax get you there? It's not a chicken and egg thing. The first word may be the thing that recalls a detail that you didn't remember. Then, the detail gets a little more attention. The language stays with the trouble. If you can stay, go deeper. If you can't, see what the house prices on Chadbourne are these days. Find out if there is still water in Stansbury Lake. Write the words feet feet feet one right after the other. What do the next words do?

Ernest Hemingway said, "There is nothing to writing. Just sit at your typewriter and bleed." I love this image, especially as I take it literally, imagining spikes on my keyboard, spiked metal eye-openers from *A Clockwork Orange* digging into my sockets, razors lining wrist rests. Figuratively, it seems a little dramatic. Most of the wounds we write about have been stitched or soldered closed. How much do we need to pick at the wound?

My friend John visited recently from Germany. Before he arrived or the dinner I hosted at my house, he attended a breathing class. He said it was the most profound experience—as intense as taking LSD. He cried until he laughed and then cried some more. "It works for trauma little t as well as Trauma big T. I think I only have little ts, like the times I've short-changed my marriage or my kids. But one kid, he was going through what might have been big T Trauma. I reached out to him and held his hand. The whole experience was like making new connections with the world. And this kid."

I believe that therapy is therapy and writing is writing, but John's experience seemed more in line with writing than therapy. There was no guide except for the man who led the breathing. The trauma wasn't being processed. It was being sat with. In *How to Plant a Billion Trees*, I refer to the eco-philosophy of Donna Haraway, as I do here. In *Staying with the Trouble*, she suggests that, in order to rethink our relationship to the world, which me must do to stave off climate change, we must not look away. As we sit in our sadness and grief at the burning, flooding, immigration-forcing, species-annihilating effects of global warming, we can catalogue all that we love and all that we will miss.

Writing is about Staying with the Trouble. It's about breathing. It's about sitting in grief and sadness and looking it straight in the face. Or, if not straight in the face, then, as Emily Dickinson declares, "Tell All the Truth/But Tell it Slant." The sheer act of sitting will deepen your voice. The breathing will add tone and layers. And you're the tilt of your head, the way you raise your eyebrow at a sentence that's a bit out of whack, the way that you stare so hard at the screen, little bugs seem to rush across the page. What I take from Hemingway is not so much the figurative message that writing will rip your heart right out of your chest, but the idea that your body is in play. Writing is a sport. My husband, working from home, sat next to me for four whole hours as I wrote. When we finished working, he said, "Now I see what you do all day. You talk to yourself the whole time. You make weird faces. You walk around and talk to yourself some more." I told him I should get credit on my Apple Watch for wiggling around so much. We decided to call it "core training."

Like painting, sculpting, dancing, acting, writing is an embodied art. If you sit with your body, notice its movements, feel the wind on your skin, smell the dog food factory, listen to the cars on the freeway. Here, with your own particular body in your own particular kind of place, the words you type will be your voice because they come from your blood. Denise Levertov said that a line of poetry is a breath. If you're talking about how long a line is or what word it should end on, her advice doesn't help that much. But, if you think of a breath as a thing that can only come from you, then each line of poetry, each sentence of your prose, will be effused with you.

Finding Your Voice Prompt

When I was revising *How to Plant a Billion Trees,* I needed to turn these individual, braided essays into a full-length book with a narrative arc. Although one of the narrative threads is recovering from sexual abuse and regaining autonomy, I had to be sure that the other thread, the one about trees, truly worked. I realized that where I began: after the molestation and abortion at eleven, I felt like the forest around me had burned down. Forests can recover from fire, but it depends on the heat of the fire and the ways foresters manage the burn scar. If the burn is so hot that the mycorrhizal fungi under the soil burns, the forest usually won't come back. Sometimes, it will, which we need it to in all its complexity if it's going to help absorb carbon. Some environmentalists have called for the planting of a trillion trees, with the hope that will save us. But that has its own complexities. Sometimes, paper companies replant the forest with a single fast-growing species so they can harvest the wood quickly. Is there space enough? Water enough? Knowledge enough. Is going all in with trees a safe bet?

"Trees or bust" after the molestation was my approach. Following the burn, any old tree would do. I clung to any sense of security following the molestation, including sleeping with too many people and getting stuck in relationships that didn't do any long-term good. Later, I began to understand how forests work—that it's not just trees you need but all kinds of supportive environments—especially if the forests are going to be a major force against climate change.

Climate change feels, even with the promise of a trillion trees, an intractable problem. Fighting for reproductive rights, bodily autonomy, and the way that our patriarchal culture perpetuates sexual abuse feels similarly futile. But perhaps it's the fight that matters.

In one chapter, in the middle of the book, I write about how forests can be easily decimated when climate change affects their defense systems. With drought and warmer temperatures, pine beetles chew through stacks of trees like my son Max chews through stacks of Takis. At fourteen, Max has a processed food problem. I prefer the problems of fourteen-year-olds to the problems of toddlers. At fourteen, I can easily see where the lines of the patriarchy run through him. He teases me, as when I'm driving and I hit a curb taking a right turn too hard. "Good one, mom." Or when I call, "Max. Max Max" in ever louder cadences and it's not until I hit full decibel that he says, "What?" But he also worries that he won't be tall enough to play Varsity basketball and the mom of one of the girls he has been friends with since kindergarten texted me at the beginning of his freshman year to say, "Thank Max, please, for being kind to my daughter. It's rough out there and she is lucky to have a good guy friend." He makes sure the kittens are in by 3:00 pm and he cooks for us some nights and does the dishes most. That's to say, he's been influenced, maybe even infected by patriarchal culture, but there are balancing forces working within.

In *How to Plant a Billion Trees,* pine beetles figure for the patriarchy, taking down organic systems systematically. What happened at Max's daycare felt similar to that process. The daycare operator's son, allowed to watch each of our kids, took one child into a bathroom and molested her. She had come to the daycare intact and left with an infiltrated forest. Like pine beetles, molestation spreads. It spreads through the minds of men to boys. It spreads through the boys to younger boys and girls. The pine beetles seem to know not what they do, although the effects impact little kids' lives. It's hard to escape pine-beetles. But some very studious people are at work on it.

In the essay, I want this idea to come through, but more via imagery and scene than me stating it too explicitly. I want people to feel the impact. I want to make the connections between pine beetles, forests, insects, infiltration, little kids, big kids, puberty, reproduction, wilfulness and accident. I want to make more reality of the reality I've already observed so I can understand what happened, why it happened, a little better. And perhaps we can understand it better together.

Here's an early draft.

> A perfect forest can stave off bark beetles. When you and your compatriots are thriving, bark beetles can only get a foot in the door, they can't wrench it open. A nibble here or there, the tree can stand. The bark can heal over. The cambium, softer, more susceptible to injury than bark, with enough nutrients and water running through its cellulose, can repel the insect. But as climate changes and droughts persist, the bark beetle has more leverage. It can not only wrench open the door to feed itself, but it can also keep the door open for all its cousins. Eggs are laid. The babies, when hatched, devour. Everyone is munching on the cambium now. Cellulose service is interrupted. What the ground giveth, the beetle taketh away. The needles cannot photosynthesize without water.
>
> In canyons throughout the west, forests are striped. Brown, green, brown, green. Dead. Alive. Dead. Alive. 85,000 square miles have been affected in the US 65,000 square miles in Canada. Europe's and Russia's forests have not escaped. Global warming affects the whole globe. It just doesn't get cold enough to kill them off. A researcher at the University of Utah noted that one infestation was so intense, when the beetles ran out of trees, they started attacking telephone poles. Southern pine beetles die when temperature go down to 14 below zero. But as the global temperature ratchets up, the latitude where 14 degrees Fahrenheit climbs about 40 feet per year. The beetles climb north. They survive warm winters. The trees, although they too move north, cannot outrun the bugs.[1]
>
> In a perfect society, teenage boys wouldn't molest younger girls. Why do they do it? The daycare owner's son took a five-year-old into the bathroom. He pulled down her pants and touched her vagina. Why did he do it? Opportunity? Sure. An overly sexualized media culture? Yes. A patriarchy that says, boys can get away with almost anything? Also yes. But nothing quite explains why he would hurt a five-year-old. Could he

---

1 https://e360.yale.edu/features/small-pests-big-problems-the-global-spread-of-bark-beetles.

have possibly thought she would like it? The twistedness here is as unfathomable as boys who shoot AR-15s into kindergartens and boys who grow into men to torture prisoners. It's hard to compare broken social ecosystems with broken natural ones because we have evidence of a well-balanced, perfectly harmonious forest. Whatever human history has been recorded, there's no moment where every single human had everything they needed and nothing they didn't.

And yet, hope for a utopic version of the world drives me to this question: What went wrong for this daycare owner's son, what went wrong for the babysitter, that made him think, well, this really won't be so bad for her. Or maybe physical need—for both power and sex, trumped every thought about the five-year-old. Or the ten-year-old. If I had had the tools to say what I felt, if I had told the babysitter a story about myself, maybe he would have seen me as a real person instead of a tool for his desire. If our culture valued stories as much as we value desire or power, maybe we could listen more attentively, like the trees do.

Here, there is information. There is some lilt to the voice with the staccato sentences and questions. But I can't quite see the forest and the questions I ask after thinking about the child molester—who, like my babysitter molester, was officially still a child—seem general and vague. So, using my own advice from this chapter, I dug in. I expanded. I added layers. I followed Natalie Diaz's advice to add before I deleted. I didn't use words like "upset" or "confused," but I hope I conveyed them.

A perfect forest can stave off bark beetles. When you and your compatriots are thriving, bark beetles can only get a foot in the door, they can't wrench it open. A nibble here or there, the tree can stand. The bark can heal over. The cambium, softer, more susceptible to injury than bark, with enough nutrients and water running through its cellulose, can repel the insect. Sap serves as a seal. The glaciers of newer bark make rivulets of older bark. The trunks' flaky golds and reds climb up into the green canopy that covers them like an umbrella. Who is protecting who?

I have sat under trees in a rainstorm, my back against the trunk, my feet against the roots. I measured the tops of trees, trying to remember if it was OK to sit in a grouping of trees when lightning threatened, as long as you didn't sit near the tallest one. The branches made imperfect shelter, but they shrunk the raindrops, slimming them as if through a colander.

It's dangerous enough, looking for the tree least likely to draw lightning. Next to a pine ridden with beetles, the danger comes not only from above but from all around. If lightning strikes this hollow husk of a tree, whatever protections it had against fire took off for heartier forests long ago. Even in a rainstorm, fires break out. And, the branches above my head provide no colander effect. The drops fall fat and hard directly on my head.

But then, this notion of rain. Well, years ago, it did rain. As climate changes and droughts persist, the bark beetle has more leverage. It can not only wrench open the door to feed itself, but it can also keep the door open for all its cousins. Eggs are laid. The babies, when hatched, devour. Everyone is munching on the cambium now. Cellulose service is interrupted. What the ground giveth, the beetle taketh away. The needles cannot photosynthesize without water.

In canyons throughout the west, forests are striped. Brown, green, brown, green. Dead. Alive. Dead. Alive. 85,000 square miles have been affected in the U.S. 65,000 square miles in Canada. Europe's and Russia's forests have not escaped. Global warming affects the whole globe. It just doesn't get cold enough to kill them off. A researcher at the University of Utah noted that one infestation was so intense, when the beetles ran out of trees, they started attacking telephone poles. Southern pine beetles die when temperature go down to 14 below zero. But as the global temperature ratchets up, the latitude where 14 degrees Fahrenheit climbs about 40 feet per year. The beetles climb north. They survive warm winters. The trees, although they too move north, cannot outrun the bugs.[2]

Like trees, little kids don't even know to begin to run. What is this prickling on my ankle? What is this tugging on my pantleg? Why do you put your finger between the old bark and the new bark, in the rivulets where rain sometimes collects and rushes? I should move, the little kid thinks. But then, they're covered with beetles. They're all over them and it is very hard to run when everything itches and tickles and scratches and tears.

It is harder to get inside the pine beetles' heads. It's as if they move as one. Perhaps the exactness of the touch, the way the finger fits perfectly between the old bark and the new encourages the troop of beetles to dig in deeper. It's a mob mentality. If we all go in at once, the

---

2 https://e360.yale.edu/features/small-pests-big-problems-the-global-spread-of-bark-beetles.

beetles say, we can break the defenses. The tree won't even realize what defenses it once had.

In a perfect society, teenage boys wouldn't molest younger girls. Why do they do it? The daycare owner's son took a five-year-old into the bathroom. He pulled down her pants and touched her vagina. Why did he do it? Opportunity? Sure. An overly sexualized media culture? Yes. A patriarchy that says, boys can get away with almost anything? Also yes. But nothing quite explains why he would hurt a five-year-old. Could he have possibly thought she would like it? The twistedness here is as unfathomable as boys who shoot AR-15s into grade school classrooms and boys who grow into men to torture prisoners. It's hard to compare broken social ecosystems to broken natural ones. There is evidence of a well-balanced, perfectly harmonious forest—the kind that existed before man manipulated them. Human systems seem perennially broken. For every good act, like Jimmy Carter, who worked to build houses for Habitat for Humanity, we have a Donald Trump, who appealed the verdict forcing him to pay E. Jean Carroll 5 million dollars for raping her and has been accused of other rapes, who was elected President of the United States again. The pine beetles have infested The White House.

And yet, hope for a solution—to infestation, pine beetles, molestation, climate change leads me to ask: What went wrong for this daycare owner's son? What went wrong for my babysitter? What made them think, well, this really won't be so bad for her. Or maybe physical need—for both power and sex, trumps every thought about the five-year-old or the ten-year-old.

In that daycare, the pine beetles ran along the baseboards. They sat on the handles of forks and in the curves of spoons. The beetles flew, air filters catching none of them. The daycare operator mopped every day and yet she never even noticed a single body. Or, at least that's what she said. I worry that Max breathed that air, ate off of those spoons, sat on the newly mopped floor. What part of his bark was threatened? Or, what siren song did the beetles sing to him?

What are the defenses? For pine beetles, there's the chance of a hormonal fix to their relentless chewing. I imagine a hormonal fix could work for child molesters too—even for the patriarchy at large. Less testosterone could help. But it's the system that's the problems. The pine beetles feed on each other's energy. The only way to interrupt that energy is with a different kind.

What if, in that bathroom, the little kid had said to the big kid, I want to tell you a story? What if he'd stopped his creepy crawling for long enough for her to say, Once Upon a Time, little kids knew how to run.

If I had had the tools to say what I felt, if I had told the babysitter a story about myself, maybe he would have seen me as a real person instead of a tool for his desire. If our culture valued stories as much as we value power, maybe we could listen more attentively, like the trees listen, through their mycorrhizal fungal systems, their branches, their chemical signals, to each other.

Only by adding more imagery, more interiority, and more details could I connect the physicality of the pine beetles to the physicality of the molestation without intruding on the privacy, even the privacy I keep for the girl in my own head. I found my way into figuring out what I think the problem is—a silent, but mob-like mentality, exacerbated by rapists getting away with murder—that pervades our culture. Power and sex at any cost, say the pine beetles.

I also got to imagine more deeply the difference between the healthy tree and the infested one. I felt so sad for the dying, husk of a tree. It couldn't help itself and it couldn't help me. So much of our strength comes from helping others. I wonder if that too goes for trees.

And, I had to enter a scary, unpleasant place, briefly wondering how the pine beetles affected Max, which was hard to write but necessary. We live in patriarchy land. To have a son is to cede some part of him to that. My job is to appreciate when he deviates from the sex and power motif. And my job is to tell him my story. Because I've practiced my voice, maybe he'll listen.

Finding Your Voice Prompt

Write us your story. I can't wait to read it

Notes

1 John Muir, *The Mountains of California*, Modern Library of America Edition (1997).
2 W. S. Merwin, "Scale in May," *The Lice*, anniversary ed., Copper Canyon Press (2017).

3 Donna Haraway, *Staying with the Trouble: Making Kin in the Chthulucene*, Duke University Press (2016).
4 Ibid.
5 Peter Friederici, *Beyond Climate Breakdown: Envisioning New Stories of Radical Hope*, Massachusetts Institute of Technology Press (2022).
6 Geetha Iyer, "Of Least Concern," *Territory Magazine*, https://themapisnot.com/issue-v-geetha-iyer (2017).
7 Kiese Laymon, *Heavy*, 1st ed., Scribner (2018).
8 Heidi Czerwiec, *Crafting the Lyric Essay*, Bloomsbury Publishing (2023).
9 Natalie Diaz, "They Don't Love You Like I Love You," *Postcolonial Love Poem*, Graywolf Press (2020).
10 Susan Mitchell, "Notes Toward a History of Scaffolding," John D'Agata (ed.), *The Next American Essay*, Graywolf Press (2003).
11 Czerwiec, *Crafting the Lyric Essay*.
12 Bhanu Kapil, *Humanimal: A Project for Future Children*, Kelsey Street Press (2009).
13 Ibid.
14 Ibid.
15 Catherine Loveday, "Why Are Minor Chords Sad and Major Chords Happy?," *BBC Science Focus*, https://www.sciencefocus.com/science/why-are-minor-chords-sad-and-major-chords-happy (2022).

BIBLIOGRAPHY

Askowitz, Andrea. *A Numbers Game*, Memoir Land (2024).
Bacigalupi, Paulo. *The Tamarisk Hunter*, High Country News (2006).
Champagne, Brooke. *Nola Face*, University of Georgia Press (2024).
Carlin, David. "Lyrebird in the Impasse," *Bending Genre*, 2nd ed., Bloomsbury Publishing (2023).
Carlin, David, and Nicole Walker. *The After-Normal: Brief, Alphabetical Essays on a Changing Planet*, Rose Metal Press (2019).
Christman, Jill. *If This Were Fiction: A Love Story in Essays*, University of Nebraska Press, 2022.
Czerwiec, Heidi. "Teaching Nicole Walker's 'Fish,'" https://brevity.wordpress.com/2017/10/02/teaching-brevity-nicole-walkers-fish/ (2017).
Czerwiec, Heidi. *Crafting the Lyric Essay*, Bloomsbury Publishing (2023).
Dungy, Camille. *Soil: A Black Mother's Garden*, Simon & Schuster (2023).
Fellner, Steve. "On Fragmentation," *Eating Lightbulbs and Other Essays*, Ohio State University Press (2021).
Furman, Andrew. *Of Slash Pines and Manatees*, University of Florida Press (2025).
Freiderici, Peter. *Beyond Climate Breakdown: Envisioning New Stories of Radical Hope*, Massachusetts Institute of Technology Press (2022).
Geha, Joseph. *Kitchen Arabic*, University of Georgia Press (2023).
Gray-Rosendale, Laura. *College Girl*, Excelsior Editions (2013).
Griswold, John. "The Best Kind of Entertainment," *Essay Daily* (2015).
Haraway, Donna. *Staying with the Trouble: Making Kin in the Chthulucene*, Duke University Press (2016).
Hogan, Linda. "Innocence," *Dark. Sweet: New & Selected Poems*, Coffee House Press (2014).
Hopkins, Gerard Manley. "The Windhover, To Christ Our Lord," edited by John Pick. Charles E. Merrill Publishing Company (1969).
Iyer, Geetha. "Of Least Concern," *Territory Magazine*, https://themapisnot.com/issue-v-geetha-iyer (2017).
Kapil, Bhanu. *Humanimal: A Project for Future Children*, Kelsey Street Press (2009).
Katz, Solomon H. (ed.), and William Woys Weaver (associate ed.), *Encyclopedia of Food and Culture*, Volume 1, Scribner (2003).
Kilpatrick, Lynn. *In the House*, FC2 Press (2011).
Kimmerer, Robin. "Mishkos Kenomagwen: The Teaching of Grasses," *Braiding Sweetgrass*, Milkweed Editions (2013).
Kinney, Alison. *Hood*, Bloomsbury Publishing (2015).
Laymon, Kiese. *Heavy*. Scribner (2018).
Long Soldier, Layli. *Whereas*, Graywolf Press (2017).

LeMay, Eric. *In Praise of Nothing: Essays, Memoir, and Experiments*, Emergency Press (2014).

Lenhart, Lawrence. *Backvalley Ferrets: A Rewilding of the Colorado Plateau*, University of Georgia Press (2023).

Loveday, Catherine. "Why Are Minor Chords Sad and Major Chords Happy?," *BBC Science Focus*, https://www.sciencefocus.com/science/why-are-minor-chords-sad-and-major-chords-happy (2022).

Luiselli, Valeria. *Tell Me How It Ends: An Essay in 40 Questions*, Coffee House Press (2017).

Mailhot, Theresa. *Heart Berries*, Counterpoint Press (2018).

Manguso, Sarah. *Ongoingness: The End of a Diary*, Graywolf Press (2015).

Merwin, W. S. "Scale in May," *The Lice*, anniversary ed., Copper Canyon Press (2017).

Miazga, Colin, Paul Bauman, Alastair McClymont, and Chris Slater. "Geophysical investigation of the Miła 18 resistance bunker in Warsaw, Poland," *SEG Technical Program Expanded Abstracts*: 3096–3100. https://doi.org/10.1190/segam2021-3594939.1 (2021).

Miller, Brenda. "Lions and Tigers and Bears, Oh My! On Courage in Creative Nonfiction," in *Bending Genre*, 2nd ed., edited by Margot Singer and Nicole Walker, Bloomsbury Publishing (2023).

Miller, Brenda. "Swerve," *Brevity Magazine*, https://brevitymag.com/nonfiction/swerve/ (2009).

Miller, Brenda, and Suzanne Paola. *Tell It Slant*, 3rd ed., McGraw-Hill (2019).

Muir, John. *The Mountains of California*, Modern Library of America Edition (1997).

Nelson, Maggie. *The Argonauts*, Graywolf Press (2015).

Nguyen, Viet Thanh. *The Sympathizer*, Grove Press (2015).

Norris, Maddie. *The Wet Wound*, University of Georgia Press (2024).

Paar, Lydia. *The Exit Is the Entrance*, University of Georgia Press (2024).

Rankine, Claudia. *Citizen*, Graywolf Press (2014).

Sather, Erik. Redwood Survival film, https://www.youtube.com/watch?v=h6-__Pa01oo&t=4s.

Shanahan Matonis, Megan, and Dan Binkley. "Key role of mosaic-meadows in restoration of ponderosa pine ecosystem," *Forest Ecology and Management*, Volume 411, 1: 120–31 (March 2018).

Sheldrake, Merlin. *Entangled Life: How Fungi Make Our Worlds, Change Our Minds, & Shape Our Futures*, Random House (2021).

Snyder, Rachel Louise. *Women We Buried, Women We Burned*, Bloomsbury Publishing (2023).

Tempest Williams, Terry. *Refuge*, Vintage (1992).

Thompson, KT. *Blanket*, Bloomsbury Publishing (2018).

Thompson, Cliff. *Jazz June*, University of Georgia Press (2025).

Van Der Kolk, Bessel. *The Body Keeps the Score: Brain, Mind, and Body in the Healing of Trauma*, Penguin Books (2015).

Walker, Nicole. "My Abortion at Age 11 Wasn't a Choice. It Was My Life," *The New York Times*, August 18, 2022.

Walker, Nicole. *Sustainability: A Love Story*, Ohio University Press (2018).

Walker, Nicole. *Processed Meats*, Torrey House Press (2021).

Walters, Wendy S. "Soup Can; or On Hospitality," *Yale Review*, https://yalereview.org/article/soup-can-or-hospitality (2020).

INDEX

A Clockwork Orange 145
Askowitz, Andrea 62, 74

Backvalley Ferrets: A Rewilding of the Colorado Plateau 54, 100
Beyoncé 139
Black Flag 85
Blanket 97
Braiding Sweetgrass 38

Carlin, David 28, 41
Christman, Jill 89, 97
Citizen 15, 16, 20, 72, 73, 77
College Girl 115
The Courage of Turtles 77, 78, 83, 89, 92
Crafting the Lyric Essay: Strike a Chord 105
Czerwiec, Heidi 105, 138, 139

D'Agata, John 140, 141
Diaz, Natalie 138, 149
Doyle, Brian 136, 137, 140
Dungy, Camille 101

Eating Lightbulbs and Other Essays 32
Egg 27, 94, 98, 99, 108, 109, 110, 114, 138, 139, 145
enlarging the temple 130, 137
Environment 98
Essay Daily 53, 54
The Exit Is the Entrance 55

Febos, Melissa 134
Fellner, Steve 32, 35, 42
Friederici, Peter 131
Furman, Andrew 87, 107

Gay, Roxane 134
Geha, Joseph 54
General Hospital 43, 85
Gray-Rosendale, Laura 115, 119
Griswold, John 53

Halden, Rolf 98, 100
Haraway, Donna 22, 37 130, 131, 145

Heavy 137
Hoagland, Edward 77, 78, 83, 89, 92
hózhó 131
Humanimal: A Project for Future Children 141
Hungate, Bruce 62, 89

increase the available reality 55, 94, 127
"Innocence" 38, 39
Iyer, Geetha 135, 136

Kapil, Bhanu 141
Kimmerer, Robin Wall 38, 40, 41, 42
Kitchen, Judith 141

Laymon, Kiese 137
LeMay, Erik 120
Lenhart, Lawerence 54, 100
Long Soldier, Layli 48, 49
Luiselli, Valeria 48, 49, 50

Mailhot, Theresa 134
McPhee, John 83, 84, 89
Predator: A Movie, a Memoir, an Obsession 99
Maps 139
The Men We Reaped 118
Merwin, W. S. 128, 135
Miller, Lulu 99
Miller, Brenda 41, 45, 113, 115, 119, 124, 143
Mom 47, 60, 63, 65, 67, 68, 71, 79, 114, 116, 124, 125, 134, 143, 147
Monson, Ander 99
Multiply/Divide: On the American Real and Surreal 106

Nguyen, Viet Thanh 31, 35, 42, 85, 86, 87, 89, 92
Nomeansno 7, 45

Of Slash Pines and Manatees: A Highly Selective Guide to My Suburban Wilderness 87

Paar, Lydia 55
Philip, Leila 100
Rankine, Claudia 50, 57

resistance 15, 16, 20, 72, 73, 77
Rich, Adrienne 6

Salt Lake City 3, 7, 16, 18, 58
Sather, Max 11, 12, 13, 14, 23, 147, 151, 152
Sather, Zoë 23, 47, 116, 125
Soil 101
Snyder, Rachel Louise 134
St. Augustine 7, 70

Tell Me How It Ends 48, 49, 50
Tempest Williams, Terry 58
The After Normal 28, 29, 41

The New York Times 2, 5, 6, 16, 17, 20, 47
Thompson, Cliff 54, 82
Thompson, KT 97
Top Chef 7
tree 16, 21, 22, 23, 25, 37, 38, 40, 42, 58, 62, 63, 67, 75, 78, 79, 84, 92, 97, 108, 114, 130, 132, 133, 134, 144, 145, 145, 147, 148, 149, 150, 152
trouble 5, 7, 16, 22, 25, 30, 32, 37, 43, 66, 72, 86, 88, 91, 130, 131, 135, 143, 145

Wallace, David Foster 81
Walters, Wendy S. 106
Ward, Jesmyn 118, 124
Why Fish Don't Exist
Wiel, Simone 136
Women We Loved, Women We Buried 134